The Geography of God's Incarnation

The Geography of God's Incarnation

Landscapes and Narratives of Faith

Ann M. Pederson

Foreword by
Philip Hefner

CASCADE *Books* • Eugene, Oregon

THE GEOGRAPHY OF GOD'S INCARNATION
Landscapes and Narratives of Faith

Copyright © 2013 Ann M. Pederson. All rights reserved. Except for brief quotations in critical publications or reviews, no part of this book may be reproduced in any manner without prior written permission from the publisher. Write: Permissions, Wipf and Stock Publishers, 199 W. 8th Ave., Suite 3, Eugene, OR 97401.

All biblical quotations are from the Common English Bible.
Common English Bible, copyright @. All rights reserved.

Cascade Books
An Imprint of Wipf and Stock Publishers
199 W. 8th Ave., Suite 3
Eugene, OR 97401

www.wipfandstock.com

ISBN 13: 978-1-61097-299-4

Cataloguing-in-Publication data:

Pederson, Ann.

    The geography of God's incarnation : landscapes and narratives of faith / Ann M. Pederson ; foreword by Philip Hefner.

    xxvi + 162 pp. ; 23 cm. Includes bibliographical references.

    ISBN 13: 978-1-61097-299-4

    1. Spiritual Life—Christianity. 2. South Dakota—Civilization—20th century. 3. Montana—Civilization—20th century. 4. Incarnation. 5. Creation. 6. Sacred space. I. Hefner, Philip, J. II. Title.

BV895 .P43 2013

Scriptures marked (NRSV) come from New Revised Standard Version Bible, ©1989, Division of Christian Education of the National Council of the Churches of Christ in the United States of America. Used by permission. All rights reserved.

Scriptures marked (CEB) come from the Common English Bible ©2011 Common English Bible.

Manufactured in the U.S.A.

For Gary, my husband and muse,
who has always helped me to find my way in life.
For Byron, Jack and the Mother Queen—my
companions on many trips to Beaver Creek.

Contents

Foreword by Philip Hefner | ix
Preface: A Geography of God's Incarnation | xiii
Acknowledgments | xxv

1 To Know Who We Are, We Must Know Where We Are | 1
2 The Spiritual Significance of Place | 16
3 An Incarnational Methodology | 33
4 Grounding Incarnation in Creation | 49
5 Incarnation at the Crossroads | 78
6 The Incarnational Marks of the Church | 112
7 We End Where We Began | 144

Bibliography | 157

Foreword

"To start my journey, I will share the most fundamental thing I know about being human: my location." With these words, Ann Milliken Pederson introduces us to The Geography of God's Incarnation. Readers should be aware, however, that this book is not just one thing—its joy lies in the fact that it falls into several genres at once.

It delights as a personal memoir. You will know Ann Pederson better when you follow her accounts of the journeys—should we say rather the pilgrimages—that have been important to her. We get a feel for the expanses of the Dakotas and Montana, but also for particularities of place and the energy of her commitment to those places: following the trail to a prospector's cabin for conversation and grub and constructing a new foundation for the cabin; searching out a forgotten memorial to an asylum for mentally ill Indians—in the middle of a present-day golf course in South Dakota—as well as a medical research center; not to forget the Roadkill Café. This stunning western territory is also the home of men and women and children, and the author is insistent that we meet them. Animals are here too, above all Jack, the standard poodle, and Byron, the poodle-cross, who are constant companions—and the cloned cows of the Trans Ova Genetics institute in northwestern Iowa, kin to both the poodles and (by genetic manipulation) their human companions. The geography in this book's title is a very personal geography, and it is both landscape and people. It is a cultural geography, Ann Pederson's own cultural geography.

In Pederson's hands, *place* becomes a very thick concept, not only a geographical location but "a dialectical relationship between environment and human narrative"[1]; "place is space that has the capacity to be remembered and to evoke what is most precious."[2] Our place can convey

---

1. See this volume, page 18.
2. Sheldrake, *Spaces for the Sacred*, 1; quoted in this volume, page 18.

Foreword

us to disease and oppression, even as it gives shape to how we hear God's word and how we work out our life's vocation. There is nothing sentimental here; this is not your grandmother's sense of place; it is inhabited by many creatures, including the human and nonhuman transgenic and transcultural hybrids, just as it is in part technonature governed by *technosapiens*.

We have here also an original contribution to our thinking about method in doing Christian theology. To be more specific, we find in this book a proposal for interpreting the Christian faith—in technical terms, a hermeneutical proposal that centers on the actuality of place. I state it thus: an adequate interpretation of Christian faith must on the one hand bring place—location—into the heart of our theology and on the other hand throw fresh light on what place means for us and for God. This method embraces a two-way traffic: place must make an impact on our theology, and our theology must make an impact on our understanding of place.

The reflections on personal places that figure so large in this book set the stage for Ann Pederson's governing concept of place. In following her over the terrains of her life, we get a sense for what she means when she writes, "places are made from the relationships that people have with them."[3] Her concept of place is terrain, no doubt about that, whether it is the mountains and valleys of Montana, the plains of South Dakota, the streets of Chicago, or the historic landmarks of Great Britain. But it is terrain that has entered into her mind and soul, terrain that stands in relationship to her. She loves to cite her "favorite aphorism of . . . Whitehead's" to the effect that "when I enter a room I don't say, 'Hello, . . . I brought my body with me.'"[4] Reading this book, we come to understand that the body she brings with her includes her place(s); she does not carry this body with her, as in a briefcase—this body of places and her relationships to them *is* Ann Pederson. When she enters a room, all of this enters with her: body, place, self. She challenges us to understand how we all join her; every one of us is an embodied and located self.

What makes this a principle for interpretation? Just this: that just as the interpreter is a self composed of body-place relationships, so her interpretations, whether of the Bible, classic faith and theology, poetry, history, politics, or science should throw light on those relationships and be clarified by them. "Bodies and places come together in

---

3. See this volume, p. 151.
4. Ibid. 151.

Foreword

incarnation."[5] Place is what God created, as well as what God came to dwell in through incarnation.

In this volume, the hermeneutic is applied theologically to the doctrines of creation, the image of God, and the incarnation. God did not originally create the world in the abstract but concretely, as a constellation of particular places, and God's continuing creation works grace in these places. It is not enough to say that we are created as individuals contained in our own skins, or that we are individuals in relationship to other persons. Since God created us as located and embodied persons, our identity as selves resides outside us in our world as much as within our individual bodies. It follows that the image of God in which we are created is a shared image that in turn shares in the mystery of God. All creation has been created in the image of God, including all particular places.

The hermeneutic of place breaks open our understanding of God's incarnation in Jesus Christ in fundamental ways. Augmenting her interpretation with insights from Eastern Orthodox theologians, Pederson draws upon Philip Sherrard's concept of the universality of the incarnation, in which God assumed not simply a human body, but "the totality of human nature, mankind as a whole, creation as a whole."[6] Here we get a sense of the largeness of the canvas on which Pederson paints and why she says of location that it is "the most fundamental thing I know about being human."[7] Theological readers will recognize that these proposals are far reaching; they call for exciting reformulations of traditional doctrines, opening up refreshing new vistas.

Personal memoir, reflection on place, hermeneutical proposal, rethinking basic Christian doctrine—and yet one more genre awaits us in the pages that follow: an integration of current scientific research into theological thinking. The research is cutting-edge cognitive science as it focuses on what is called extended mind or situated cognition. As she delves into this new field, which is just taking shape, Pederson shows what difference science can make for our thinking, and how it opens new avenues for understanding our lives and our faith. Her approach fashions a seamless whole. Neither the science nor the theology is simply tacked on as an appendage; each is integral to the whole understanding. We have a model here of how theology should relate to science.

5. Ibid. 151.
6. Quoted from Knight, *The God of Nature*, in this volume, p. 150.
7. See this volume, p. 3.

Reading this book is to take the journey with Ann Pederson. We will follow our own maps, so our journeys and our places will not be identical to hers or to each other's. But we learn from this book what journeys and places are all about, and we find ourselves compelled to engage their spiritual depth.

Philip Hefner

Preface
A Geography of God's Incarnation
Narratives and Landscapes of Faith

While I started writing this book on sabbatical, this project is actually the result of reflecting on my lifelong love of going on journeys: on foot as I hiked through the mountains of Montana, driving in a CRV with my husband and two dogs through the landscapes of the Dakotas and upper Great Plains, going on retreats to a nearby Benedictine Abbey in Minnesota, visiting the great cathedrals and pubs in England, sitting in my backyard watching the birds. To places nearby and far away. The geographies of my life are also the geographies of my Christian faith, and this project has led me to make connections between them, and to see that where I've been and will go in the future is as important to my understanding of the Christian faith as who, what, and when. Ultimately, the who, what, when, and where cannot be separated. For me, they are all connected with the why—to the great questions about the meaning of life and our relationship to God in all of it. Theology is about making connections between the where and the what and who of the Christian faith. It's about trying to make sense of the Christian claim that the Word becomes flesh and dwells among us.

FROM ROSEANNE KELLER

"Pilgrimage ultimately is a journey leading through the geography of our own hearts."[1]

---

1. Keller, *Pilgrim in Time*, 2.

Preface

FROM BILL BRYSON

"I was in a part of the world where you could drive hundreds of miles in any direction before you found civilization, or at least met another person who didn't like accordion music."[2]

FROM JOHN STEINBECK

"A journey is a person in itself; no two are alike. And all plans, safeguards, policing, and coercion are fruitless. We find after years of struggle that we do not take a trip; a trip takes us."[3]

FROM PHILIP SHELDRAKE

"*Peregrination,* or pilgrimage for Christ, may be said to be central to Celtic spirituality."[4]

These quotations express the heart of what it means to be on a journey, to take a road trip. This book is about one such road trip, one in which I explore how landscapes and place are at the heart of my understanding of God's incarnation in the world. It is no surprise to Christians that the center of the incarnation is the person of Jesus Christ—God in flesh made manifest. But it might be a stretch for some Christians to imagine that the good news that God, the Word, has become flesh is not only in a person but also in a particular place—in creation. This world, where we are in the here and now, manifests God's commitment to be fully present in the places of our lives. And this world is our home, God's home. I love the translation from the Common English Bible of the classic text from John 1:14: "The Word became flesh and *made his home* among us." No matter where we are in our life, God is at home in us. This project explores the road trips of our lives and journeys we take to places nearby and far away, while also realizing that as we go on life's expeditions simultaneously we are at home in God and God in us.

2. Bryson, *The Lost Continent,* 293.
3. Steinbeck, *Travels with Charley,* 3.
4. Sheldrake, *Living Between Worlds,* 58.

Preface

My question for this book and my life is, what does geography or place have to do with the incarnation of God and with our spiritual lives as Christians? I have come to realize that my Christian faith has been formed, not only by the people in my life, but also by the places in which I have lived and traveled. The heart of my faith is buried in the mystery that the God who created this world is the same God who is incarnate in this world. And I have been trying to understand and explain these beliefs for most of my life. That's why I love theology. For most Christians, incarnation means first and foremost that God has come to this world in the person of Jesus Christ. I would call this an incarnational faith of the second article, a christological focus that begins with Jesus Christ and then moves to the rest of creation. Surely the incarnation of God in Christ is important to my understanding of the Christian faith, but it is important in so far as this person of Christ is the one through whom God has created the whole world. The creation is the home of my theological framework, the foundation on which I understand everything else. Creation in a sense is the *where* of God's incarnation and Jesus Christ is the *who*. This might be a bit simplistic, but the Christian tradition, especially in recent times, has concentrated so exclusively on the person of Christ that it has forgotten the *where* of God's action. We will explore in later chapters why I think the Christian tradition has been ambivalent about both place and geography as central metaphors for interpreting theological doctrines.

My conviction is that the geographies of our lives are as fully an expression of God's incarnation in the world as are the people and other creatures with whom we share this world. I am a theologian and professor by trade, and also a lover of travel—both to the local places and to the far-flung corners of the world. With this volume my hope is to provide those who accompany me on this journey with a kind of road map, or at least with occasional markers, through the geographical cartography of the Christian faith. As we stop to notice historical markers on the side of the road, we will pull over on the wayside and pay attention to the stories and details that are often forgotten and are often simply ignored or driven by. We will notice the giant road signs telling us what is ahead of us, and where we have been along the way. At other points, we will take the detours. Like cairns on the trails above the timberline, these theological markers help us to traverse the Christian faith, to help find our place in this crazy world, and to understand how this planet Earth in its tragic

Preface

beauty is our home, a home in which God promises not only to be present with us now but also in the future.[5]

I began this journey and project while I was on sabbatical two years ago. Before that, I spent the year as the interim campus pastor, filling in for the pastor, who was on sabbatical in Africa. Since my first year of teaching, I didn't remember being so tired as I was when I filled in for the campus minister. The days were filled, and mostly I loved it. I thrived on it, actually. But at the end of the academic year, I was ready for sabbatical. Facing a sabbatical year when all of a sudden days weren't filled with appointments seemed like a future filled with endless possibilities. I imagined I would start the day with a cup of Irish Breakfast tea, read in the sunroom, leisurely write for a few hours, walk the dogs, and end the day dining with my husband. He would return from work and ask me what I had accomplished. I would read from my manuscript. Idyllic days were ahead. However, the time didn't unfold exactly like I planned or hoped. I went from feast to famine: hardly any appointments and deadlines were self-imposed. Suddenly, I was empty and anxious. I was faced with a different kind of geography: the space of my own restlessness. It dawned on me yet again that one of the places in which I have the most trouble being at home was with myself and with God. I had faced mixed emotions about the vast expanses of the prairie, but I now faced a different kind of ambivalence within myself and with God. I was displaced from my usual routine and surroundings (my office and work). Where would I go to quell this restlessness? Well, I had already decided I was too tired to go to Europe or run off to Africa. I needed to stay home, and if I decided to travel, it must be on a pilgrimage to the near, the close by. And that is exactly what happened.

Sabbatical unfolded into a journey to the small places. I didn't need to go abroad or to some exotic location to find what I needed this time for rest and recreation. I've always been one who wants to be on the run, going somewhere, never really at rest. For much of my life that has been a good thing. But for this time, I needed to stay put to find those places in my life that I could only attend to when I was closer to home and paying attention. Even now, after my sabbatical has ended, I realize how difficult it is for me to rest, to let in that deep peace, the kind that renews and restores. I will always be one who has trouble staying still. Psalm 46:10, "Be still and know that I am God," has never been my favorite Bible verse!

---

5. Revelation 21:1–3 (NRSV).

Preface

But I tried nonetheless to pause, to find the detours, to stop along the way. During these last two years, I have discovered that the small and local out-of-the way places, the weekly rituals, and the casual and unexpected discussions I have encountered have enriched me beyond measure. I am deeply grateful for the way in which I am learning to be at home again. I will always be restless; it's part of my genetic makeup. But now I know that I can also be at home within that restlessness. This recent sabbatical helped me reflect more deeply on the geographies of my Christian faith—my journey both within the world at large and within my own soul. If I look back over the year and think about where I've been, I think about all the pictures I've taken of the same trees, the same nature preserve through which I hiked, and the same art studio I went to week after week. And yet these places were never the same. They have been changing along with me, and the miracle is I've learned to notice those changes.

As I reflect back on my own theological upbringing, I realize how important the notion of place has been for the formation of my beliefs. Several places in my life have been the vehicles of God's grace, sacramental geographies, if you will. They convey and carry me through the relationships that I experience in those locations. Places are not containers or simply backdrops I go to. Rather they are the connections between processes, people, patterns, practices, and perceptions that make up that place. I have hiked in the forest-covered mountains of Montana, attended chapel at the Lutheran seminary in urban Chicago, worshiped at Christ Church in Oxford, England, meandered through the woods of Beaver Creek Nature Preserve in South Dakota, and wandered around the grounds of St. John's Abbey in Collegeville, Minnesota. Though the places are vastly different, my experiences of them hold some things in common. They are simultaneously places of radical immanence and transcendence, of feeling at home and yet being on the way, of solitude and intense community, of order and adventure, of beauty and tragedy.

Hiking in the forests of Montana brings these contradictions together into a kind of productive tension. Every spring I succumb to the same ritual of listening to a certain piece of music that is one of my favorites, because it carries me to places I love. I can't listen to *Appalachian Spring* by Aaron Copland without getting a serious case of wanderlust. From almost nowhere, the strings slowly and quietly enter, as if in diffused light. The clarinet joins the quiet, almost melancholic opening. I know that Copland did not compose this famous opus about a Montana forest, but every time I hear it, I'm transported into a thick

Preface

stand of lodgepole pines, their pungent odor accompanying the scene. Every spring I listen to this piece several times. As happens when I look through the photographs of an old scrapbook, I'm flooded with memories, a longing to return to my native home, and a poignant realization that I will likely never again make Montana my home. Yet, those mountains will always be my first spiritual home. I carry something of them inside me. Whether it's traveling to Wyoming and Montana each summer or facing the prairie horizon as the sun is setting, I love facing west. With some irony, I remember that Per Hansa, the main character in the epic prairie novel, *Giants in the Earth*, by O. E. Rolvaag, is found in the spring, frozen to death from exposure in a winter blizzard, facing westward. Whenever I face west, as prairies undulate into mountains, for me, home is not yet found. I will always face westward, toward the horizons which pull me beyond prairie sunsets to the forests of Montana and to all the places where I will relentlessly search for answers and never find them. Finding my home is recognizing the tireless inquiry that leads me to God. I love the daily rhythm of looking westward, of watching setting suns on a distant horizon while knowing that another day will come.

These experiences are the rhythms of faith: they give our life order when we are in chaos; they provide hope when we are in deep despair; they provide a way when there seems to be no way through it all. In all of these settings, I am simultaneously a recipient of grace from all those who surround me and an active participant in the journey of their faith. When I hike with my dogs at Beaver Creek Nature Preserve, I really believe that the blue jays that fly through the bush or the deer that dart across the path worship God with me, adding their own unique voice. I "get" the Psalms differently when I hike in the woods than when I sing them responsively in church. I can now hear the praises sung from "mountains and all hills, fruit trees and all cedars! Wild animals and all cattle, creeping things and flying birds."[6] The music of creation is a doxological symphony to the creator.

Our relationships with creatures both human and nonhuman help us practice the rhythms of the world around us. These rhythms signify the movements of the Christian faith. These places I know and love simultaneously provide sanctuary and safe harbor while also sending me on ventures of which I cannot see the ending. The restlessness that marks so much of my own life needs to be countered by the safe harbor of

---

6. Psalm 148:9–10 (NRSV).

community and ritual. These places do that for me. And yet, I am never at home in such a way that I simply remain there, unchanged or unmoved. Instead I also experience the intense passion and adventure of moving outward and away, of being part of church, the *ekklesia*, a community called out from itself and into the world. When I am at home in God, I am also most eager to be "on the way." I believe this is the better movement of the Christian faith: being at home enough in God's grace in order to be on the way. The Christian faith happens at this intersection of home and on the road, of on earth and in heaven. I was raised in Montana—my earthly home and a slice of heaven. (Just ask any Montanan, and they will tell you that.)

Growing up in Montana and attending summer church camp, I had an intuitive sense that where I was had to be as important as who I was—in fact, they seemed inseparable. I remember singing a camp song with words about where one could see God alive in the creation, and yet I remember at the same time being told by some pastors that it was only in Christ that I could find the true presence of God. If that was the case, then I wondered if creation didn't really matter all that much. And that seemed to go against everything I had experienced. In an odd way, this realization of dissonance between how I experienced God and what I was told about God might have been an impetus to kick-start an early career interest in theology. I wanted to prove to myself and to those pastors of my youth that what they told me wasn't true, or at least it wasn't the whole truth and nothing but the truth. I knew that creation mattered to God, and that this creation is where God lived and loved me.

When I was at Montana State University, I took my first philosophy course and was introduced to the writings of Alfred North Whitehead, who emphasized "location" as a philosophical category. I found my first philosophical and theological home: Whitehead's language helped me to find my place in the world. Later when I went to Luther Seminary, I studied Whitehead and process theology, and read the theology of Martin Luther. Only now can I put together the connection between my love of place and my interest in the incarnation and embodiment. These were joined together in the odd juxtaposition of Whiteheadian metaphysics and a Lutheran theology of creation. I would later use Whitehead's critique of 'simple location' to build my metaphysical house, in which I would first feel at home. Whitehead claimed that location is not some simple spot, a container in which we move. This would assume, he noted, that our world is nonrelational—an idea that goes against our experience of it. For Whitehead, place, time, and bodies are inseparable. We see the world with our eyes; we hear the world with our ears. We know our place in the world *with* and *through* our bodies, as our body-selves create practices and habits *with* the places around and in them. *Place* = bodies, events, processes, habits, and histories.

I have also loved the prose of Annie Dillard and the novels of Norman Maclean—both of whom emphasize the role of place in spirituality. However, it wasn't until I was in seminary when I read the theology of Joseph Sittler that I felt most at home in my own Lutheran tradition. It was Sittler's words that helped me to put into more sophisticated theological language what I had always believed. In the 1950s and 1960s, Joseph Sittler had already become an ecumenical and ecological theologian. His style was evocative, not prescriptive. He relied on the arts, poetry, and architecture for his theological inspiration almost as much as he relied on Scripture. His style of prose meandered, and he admitted that he was not a systematic thinker. I have always thought of his writings as springboards—places from which to jump into and take off on further theological adventures and explorations. Sittler's voice was prophetic; he warned us that our home, this planet, is in peril. At no other time in history have humans had such power to destroy the home in which they live. Sittler listened to scientists, read the poets, and watched the cultural signs. He warned us because he loved and celebrated the earth that God created. Instead of telling me to feel guilty about how I lived, he provoked me to think about the beauty of this world—in all of its joy and tragedy—and to save this world, because I was motivated by its beauty, and not because I was compelled by guilt. Friends of Sittler recall the Christmas Eves he would attend Augustana Lutheran Church in Chicago's Hyde Park when he would bring the finest bottle of wine for the celebration of the Eucharist. He believed that God so loved this world that we should respond in kind. He was also sensitive to those in the world who did not find it to be a hospitable place in which to live or experience God's grace. Sittler reminded me that this earth in which I live is my home, because it is also God's home.

Knowing why we are at home is crucial to self-understanding and to understanding our relationship with God. And yet many people feel like they live in a kind of no-man's land, a spiritual and social wasteland that promises to be everyone's place but in fact includes no one in particular. We have become dislocated from our families, traditions, and cultures. More and more, people are becoming displaced, dislocated, and homeless. Unlike Dorothy in *The Wizard of Oz,* many can't claim that "there's no place like home." Even for those people who have a roof over their heads, food to eat, and clothing to wear, the world has become a hostile place and an isolating place. Many of us leave from our garage in the morning, enter the workplace, and return home in the evening never meeting another person with whom we have a lasting or significant relationship. Our world spins with multiple experiences and encounters. The place that once seemed secure seems re-placed by unfamiliar markers and disorienting surroundings. We long for home yet have trouble finding it. So we must find our way home.

What we urgently need at the beginning of the twenty-first century is a theological map that can give us direction and locate a new and powerful way of helping us to interpret our place within the universe, our home in God's world. We experience and interpret the world around us through geographies, locations, and particulars of our life stories. Who we are depends on where we are and where we've come from. Christianity is passed on through the faith of our elders, the stories we tell, the hymns we memorize, the rituals we learn. To understand why we are lost in the world, we must look back at the landmarks of our faith. We need to find new ways of telling stories and making our way in the world.

I propose a theology of place. A reinvigorated theology of place/home can relocate the way we traverse and interpret the Christian faith by doing the following:

1. Relocating the incarnation of God's saving grace "on earth as it is in heaven," as well as in the new heaven and new earth yet to be;

2. Correcting the one-sided emphasis of time, progress, event, and history that is used to explain the incarnation of God; moving from the *who* to the *where*;

3. Expanding the *imago Dei* from human personhood alone to the whole of the natural order in which humans are located;

4. Providing a map to and exploration of those places where Christians have either ignored God or said God is not present;

5. Offer a spiritual antidote to the displacement and restlessness that is present in so much of our culture; and

6. Help create new trails and landmarks through the landscapes of postmodernity.

Preface

This book is primarily a theological and pastoral exploration of the Christian doctrine of the incarnation. Because the book doesn't fit neatly into categories of either systematic theology or pastoral theology, it will leave some readers dissatisfied. However, for other readers and travelers who join me on this theological exploration, the contents will lead us to some new ideas and discussions. The book is more like a springboard for discussion than a systematic theology of answers. I need to take this theological journey without worrying very much about arriving at a final destination. Too much constructive theological conversation has been thwarted by those who demand final answers instead of leaving room open for ongoing discussion and debate.

This project weaves content and method together. I claim that what we believe comes about through the practices, rituals, and experiences of our faith as much as it does through careful, systematic philosophical reflection. Hopefully, both are happening in this book at the same time. My full-time work is teaching undergraduates about Christian systematic theology, and I have no doubt that their concerns and questions are always in the back of my mind. But I also spend a lot of time with friends and colleagues for whom the Christian tradition has been an experience of either a hostile territory or a foreign land. They will also be in my mind. And finally, as an ordained Lutheran pastor, I carry with me the beliefs, rituals, doctrines, and practices of the Christian tradition. Some of them will lighten my load on this journey, while others will weigh me down. But most important, I take this journey as a means to both make sense of and find a deeper connection to this God who I, along with countless others, claim is a God who loves us enough to find a home within us.

And now we must begin the journey. Some of the old familiar landmarks of the Christian faith of our past will help guide us on our way, but we will also explore new paths and see again with new eyes these old familiar places. We might experience a geographical conversion. That is, we might find ourselves returning home to God's world, but now we will find it renewed again as we look with new eyes and a new heart. How will we get where we are going? By noticing the direction we are going, by looking ahead at the big signs that point a way, and by stopping along the way. Recently I stumbled across a website: www.waymarking.com/.[7] The description of the site reads, "Waymarking is a way to mark unique locations on the planet and give them a voice. While GPS technology

---

7. "Waymarking FAQs."

allows us to pinpoint any location on the planet, mark the location, and share it with others, Waymarking is the toolset for categorizing and adding unique information for that location. Groundspeak's slogan is 'The Language of Location' and our goal is to give people the tools to help others share and discover unique and interesting locations on the planet. We invite you to share your part of the world with us through Waymarking.com."[8] We will mark our way and hope that what we learn we can share with others about this remarkable landscape of creation—God's home in the world. And we'll add new marks, new pinpoints of information. Like punctuation marks, these markers will make us pause, question, exclaim, stop. If nothing else, as the website notes, they make us get out and notice, and take a stretch from the trip.

---

8. Ibid.

Acknowledgments

Going on road trips *are like writing books: they both take time and require good companions. To the following people and institutions, I offer my gratitude:*

To Paul R. Sponheim, Michelle Bartel, Paul Rohde, and Gary Pederson;

To my colleagues and friends who read the manuscript multiple times and made very valuable comments;

To Karie Frank, without whom I wouldn't have completed this book. She worked tirelessly at editing, typing, and making me laugh.

To Leonard Hummel, who encouraged me to write on place and whose theological work has helped me in this endeavor;

To Janet and Ross Blank-Libra, who have taught me how to "see" the prairie in all its splendor;

To Sheila Agee, whose artwork has been my hermeneutical lens for reading and interpreting God's great book of nature;

To Harry Thompson for his leadership and vision at the Center of Western Studies at Augustana College;

To Patrick Henry, who first encouraged me to start on this journey;

To the Carole Bland Grant and the Augustana College Research and Artists Funds, which provided funds for me to drive almost every mile of road in South Dakota;

To colleagues who invited me to present this material and also engaged in marvelous and challenging conversations: The Twin Cities Process and Faith Group, the Steering Committee of the Vocation of a Church College Conference, the International Society of Science and Religion, and the Advanced Seminar and Zygon Center at the Lutheran School of Theology at Chicago;

Acknowledgments

To my editor, K. C. Hanson, to my copyeditor, Jeremy Funk, and to all at Cascade Books;

Finally and most important,

To Philip Hefner, whose theological spirit and work has provided such inspiration to me. I am ever so grateful for his friendship.

1

To Know Who We Are, We Must Know Where We Are

EXCURSUS

Route 66

T̲ʜᴇ ʀᴏᴀᴅs I ʜᴀᴠᴇ *traveled this summer are not part of the famous Route 66, the "Main Street of the United States" that went from Chicago to LA. That highway was turned into a television show and became a hit song. Instead, I have toured the back roads, driving through the 66 counties of South Dakota. This summer* **South Dakota Magazine** *featured a cover with a young couple in a convertible, ready to hit the highway. Their eager smiles beckoned fellow travelers to join them. And so we did. While we don't look nearly as young or have a fancy convertible, my husband and I decided to hit the road with Jack, our standard poodle, and Byron, our poodle-cross, to see how many of these sites we could find. Such peregrinations have led us on one-lane dirt side roads near the North Dakota border, to the meandering path in the Little Bend Recreation Area along the Missouri River, and to the remote stretch of highway near the Slim Buttes. One weekend we covered nearly 1300 miles.*

What have I discovered? A landscape that still remains so vast that I don't know how to describe it. A state whose contrasts are startling: we walked

The Geography of God's Incarnation

through forest-covered hills in the southwest, looked at water stretching for miles everywhere, and grieved over tragic landscapes of poverty. Some of the poorest counties anywhere in the United States are in South Dakota. Earlier this summer we stood on the peninsula at the Little Bend Recreation Area and gazed at water all around us, Missouri River water that had spread out of its banks from the headwaters in Montana to its end in St. Louis. The vista of 2011 is one that all of us from South Dakota will remember, the chaos of waters rushing to places where we thought they'd never reach.

Gary and I stopped to read those points-of-information signs, learning about Hugh Glass (who survived a grizzly bear attack) and the Battle of Slim Buttes in September 1876. While I've learned that pilgrimages to the well known are worthwhile, I've also discovered unnoticed and forgotten places of value and loveliness. But it took a willingness to get off the beaten path. Leaving the main highways, and traveling to sights that might be least known, leaves me with a new perspective about the area in which I now live. Only when I have looked at, touched, smelled, and listened to the locations that have been forgotten or misplaced will I begin to understand where my own spot in this creation might be and how it might matter to others. I have witnessed beauty on the edges, where the suffering of the poorest is woven into landscapes of pine-covered bluffs, muddy waters, and small, dying towns. Hidden in these places is the power of God, Deus absconditus, not the hidden God who can't be trusted, but the God hidden in the opposites. God might not always be found on the main path of pilgrims, but instead God wanders on the smaller Emmaus roads, those on the map marked in blue or that are simply dotted lines. I long to go on more pilgrimages, to the unpredictable places where I might discover myriads of ways that God appears and helps people like me to notice beauty where I never thought that I could find it.

"If you don't know where you are, says Wendell Berry, you don't know who you are . . . He is not talking about the kind of location that can be determined by looking at a map or a street sign. He is talking about the kind of knowing that involves the sense, the memory, the history of a family or a tribe. He is talking about the knowledge of place that comes from working in it in all weathers, making a living from it, suffering from its catastrophes, loving its mornings or evenings or hot noons, valuing it for the profound investment of labor and feeling that you, your parents and grandparents,

your all-but-unknown ancestors have put into it. He is talking about the knowing that poets specialize in."[1]

To start my journey, I will share the most fundamental thing I know about being human: my location. I will tell you about the places from which I come. I believe that to know who I am, I must know where I am. Location is central to understanding my body-self. I experience and interpret the world around me through geographies and locations, and my place in the world connects me to my ancestors, both spiritually and genetically. Their birthplaces and graveyards are geographical extensions of my life's story. My life thus far begins in the mountains of Montana and ends on the prairies of the upper Great Plains of South Dakota. I believe that these places are where God dwells (sets up camp [John 1:14]) and lives within me. Windows from God into my world, these places reveal God's location in my world. They show me what it means to be at home in God. I begin this journey from my favorite place, the mountains of Montana.

I meander here and there. Pine trees and sun combine with the thin mountain air to create the perfect atmosphere. Whenever I smell the deep, warm scent of pine, I begin to feel at home. Home is the place that I carry within my body, even when I'm in a location where home used to be but is no longer. I haven't realized this all at once, as if in some mystical epiphany. But just as scenery appears during the hikes I've been on, unexpected insights appear from around the corners or in the shade of the trees when I take off my pack and rest for a while. So, we will wander as if on a hike up a mountain path, with lots of curves and bends, a few steep ascents, and streams to cross.

From age twelve through my first years of marriage, I returned to spend the summer at Christikon, a Lutheran camp in southern Montana. My first three summers I came as one of many campers, for a week of hiking, prayer, playing games, and making new friends in the mountainous setting. When I was a sophomore in high school, I came as a staff member, a kitchen aide. Whatever possessed the camp directors to have me work in the kitchen I will never know. I had almost flunked home economics in the ninth grade. That summer I managed to serve left-over tuna hot dish that was still partially frozen and to make a pan of brownies that even a hacksaw could not separate from the pan. The next summer I was a junior counselor. For our staff training we memorized an outline

---

1 Stegner, "Where the Bluebird Sings," 199, 205.

of the Gospel of Mark and then read *Pilgrim at Tinker Creek*, by Annie Dillard. I'm not sure that I understood all of her writing, and even today, I'm not sure I do. But its poetic and mystical-metaphysical descriptions of the natural world seemed to match my own at some level. My camp director, Stan West (who has now become a nationally celebrated author), encouraged me to read my other favorite writers as a way of studying the human condition: John Steinbeck (*East of Eden*) and Graham Greene (*The Power and the Glory*). Those stories stayed with me, and after I went to seminary and later completed a PhD in theology, I required students of mine to read the same books. From early in my childhood, I had learned to love literature of all kinds, especially fiction. My mother would read to me when my dad was at work in the evening at the airport (he was an air-traffic controller). As the years progressed, we read aloud to each other the short stories of Flannery O'Connor, the plays of Tennessee Williams, and poetry by Robert Frost.

Christikon became a second home for me. Every school year I waited and waited until I could head up the Boulder River road and begin my summer at camp. The road, infamous for its large boulders and deep ruts, twists and turns south from Big Timber, Montana. In the early 1970s, McLeod, Montana, was still big enough to have a small grocery store and a post office. The local bar, which would later be a camp staff hangout, sported chainsaws on the walls for decoration. We would stop at the little store to buy pop and candy, and to pick up the camp mail. Mail delivery was usually three times a week, delivered by the same man in the same truck, year after year. We would watch eagerly every Tuesday, Thursday, and Friday for that mail truck and then run down the rocky road to the mailbox and bring it back for all to open. It was a thrill to get a letter, and if we got three or more on one day, we would have to sing for those precious epistles before they were given to us.

I wasn't a very athletically inclined kid and was on the short side. I had no idea how much my physical endurance would be tested. I learned how to help cut down dead lodge pole pines, carry them on my shoulders back to camp or load them into the camp truck, scrape the logs, soak them in creosote, and dig post holes for them to be placed in. Over about three summers, the campers and staff built the split-rail fence that surrounded the camp's property and marked the property line. After a hard day's work, we would collapse into bed in our cabins, which often harbored visitors—marmots and mice. The lights went out, all at the same time. The camp was run by a generator in its early years, which was turned off at night. By the early to mid seventies, power lines were being laid up the Boulder River canyon. Once again, campers were recruited with staff, and we dug trenches using our hands, #10 cans, and a few shovels. The shovels were generally a nuisance; they didn't work well on the giant boulders that had to be unearthed and dragged away. We formed teams and competed to see who could get their trench done first. The trench digging was often followed by cleaning up in the creek. Mud fights and dunking each other in the cold stream were great fun and a refreshing relief after the work in the hot mountain sun. Then there was the hiking. I had grown up in the Gallatin Valley in Bozeman, Montana. I had done some hiking as a kid, but not a great deal. That changed. By the time I was in eighth grade, I discovered my favorite trail and from then on I spent every chance I could hiking up to see Charlie, the prospector.

Charlie Rasnick was probably about seventy when I first got to know him. He had settled in the Boulder canyon in the earlier part of the twentieth century as a prospector and trapper. After his marriage ended, he built a small cabin up on Bridge Creek, about one and a half miles from the Boulder road. He kept his pink and white pickup hidden in the pines near the road. For the first years, he spent the winter down at another camp, doing maintenance for them in return for room and board. Eventually, Charlie tired of the evangelical religious atmosphere (that seemed to be part of the package he didn't want), and so he began to live year round up on Bridge Creek. His own cabin was small, one room. Despite his seeming love of living like a hermit, Charlie enjoyed having company, and so he built a guesthouse out of the local lodge pole pines. It had two rooms, the kitchen/entry and the back sleeping area. I have no idea how a large, old cast-iron stove was carried up there, but it served its function by providing a place for us to cook the fried spam and potatoes that Charlie loved so much. Breakfasts were usually toast with apple sauce and condensed milk poured over the top. Pancakes with freshly picked huckleberries were a treat during the later part of the summer. Several of the staff, including me, developed a close friendship with Charlie, and we hiked up there almost every break. We'd cook for Charlie and stay overnight at the guest cabin. Because his cabin was up higher than the camp, and out of the deep canyon, he could get radio reception. We would listen to baseball games or Mystery Theater. The night would close with turning off the kerosene lamp, a quick trip to the outhouse, and a well-deserved rest in a warm sleeping bag.

The trail up to Charlie's was one of the first hikes for campers. The Bridge Creek trailhead pointed its way to Bridge Lake and Meatrack Trail. The first mile twisted steeply up through the woods, about a thousand feet in elevation. Once on top, we would walk over to the cliffs where we could look out over the canyon. I never got too close to the edge. The vertigo that has developed throughout my life was in its infancy stage back then. When we returned to the path, which had leveled out a bit, we walked the last three quarters of a mile or so and dropped down to Charlie's cabin. The trail continued beyond Charlie's for about seven miles, up to Bridge Lake and Crow Mountain. Carrying a full pack up that trail always meant sweating profusely and breathing quickly. The campers would get excited and run back and forth, wanting to hurry the trip along, but eventually the trail caught up to them, and they would find the air thinning and their capacity for running diminished. I learned to hike the steep terrain down from Charlie's cabin: slowly, placing one foot in front of the other, locking my knee. One could keep going a long way like that, inhaling, exhaling, and taking one step at a time. Now in my middle years, I could stand to relearn that lesson—this time not only for hiking but also for life.

Charlie's small family lived in West Virginia. He had a son who would occasionally visit every couple years, but he had no one nearby to whom he could pass on his love of prospecting. Several of the staff members, including me, were eager to discover what he knew about prospecting. So in the mid to late 1970s, we set off with Charlie to stake out a mining claim about two miles up on the War Eagle Trail. The area was mined in the late 1800s and then mined again during the early twentieth century. An old cabin that had been used by prospectors and trappers was still in relatively good shape. It was simply known to us as the "claim cabin." We carried large ropes, a compass, shovels, and a few other tools up the trail to the claim cabin. It took a few trips and several days, but together with Charlie, we climbed up and down the mountainside with the ropes, marking the four corners of the claim and blazing trees with an ax for the boundaries. Then when the paperwork was returned from the Bureau of Land Management, we stuck the papers in a glass jar and nailed it to a tree. We cleaned up the cabin, and for the first time several of us slept in it. We held our flashlights close to the floor that night, and watched as multiple pairs of eyes raced across the floor. Mice, lots of them. And we could hear the coyotes howling in the canyon. That was usually when the sheepherders were up in the meadows. The local ranchers from Big

Timber would pasture the sheep in the high mountain meadows during the summer months. I remember one young woman who served as cook and hired hand to the sheepherders. I thought she was really cool and that maybe someday I could do the same. I still have the letter from her that she wrote for Charlie during one Christmas.

One summer Charlie decided that the claim cabin needed some work, and so he enlisted me, Gary (my new husband), and a few other staff members to put new support logs under the main frame of the cabin. Once again my limited knowledge of cutting down pine trees came in handy. We cut down poles for the support logs. We hauled up an old jack, putting it under the corners of the building. Eventually, the cabin was elevated, the old logs taken out, and the new ones put into place. My old overalls and red bandana were the uniform of choice for those summers. I don't think I've ever worked so hard physically, to the point where placing one foot in front of the other took great effort. I'm not sure if I would have made it the two miles back to Charlie's cabin had it not been for the promise of fried spam and potatoes. My brief stint as a Montana prospector ended when, a few summers later, the area was incorporated into the Absaroka-Beartooth Wilderness Area. Charlie died, alone in his cabin, in the winter of 1981. I haven't been up there a lot since then. The Forest Service received so many petitions from past campers and staff that they agreed to leave his cabin on the wilderness land. Otherwise it would have been burned.

Charlie would occasionally talk about religion. He tended to like the Lutherans; they didn't feel a great need to proselytize like those at the other camps. But in general, he distrusted pastors and could never understand some of the things we did at camp—like having to return from hiking by a certain time. Our camp director wanted to know where the groups hiked to, and when they would return, all in the name of safety! But Charlie felt that this practice ignored the rhythm of the day and of the land. Sometimes when he would come with me and my group on our exploration of old mining tunnels up on War Eagle Mountain, he would purposely lead us far enough out and be gone long enough that we couldn't return until near sunset. But it always seemed worth it. One time we hiked up to the War Eagle tunnel, and a few of us crawled back into the darkness. I have an old photo of me emerging out of the mine shaft, red bandana, overalls, and a big smile.

I learned to hike those trails not only by sight but also by sound and smell and feel. I knew every twist and turn by heart. Oddly I felt more comfortable on those trails than I did down at the camp. One time I was coming down by myself from the claim cabin and I heard a rustle to the side of me. There was a small moose calf and in the distance; the cow was looking protectively at the calf and askance at me. I sat down and waited for what seemed like an eternity, though I'm sure it was only about thirty minutes. Eventually the duo disappeared into the woods. The woods of Montana were where I learned the most about my own faith, not in the Lutheran church where I grew up. In general, I still share the same suspicion of pastors that Charlie harbored. As an ordained Lutheran pastor, I'm even suspicious of myself. Like the early Christian patristic writers, I believe that creation, along with the Scriptures, is the revelation of God. These church fathers claimed that there were two books of faith: nature and the Bible. During my formative summers, faith was an adventure, and my knowledge of the Christian faith was supplemented by reading lots of great literature and hard physical work. While I am not a poet, I began to understand the kind of knowing that Wallace Stegner writes about, when I realized that the fence I had helped to build, the post holes I had dug with an old #10 can, were contributions I had made to this place that I loved so much. When I return each summer, as I drive up the Boulder River Road, I know that I have left something of myself in that canyon.

I no longer dig post holes or climb into mining tunnels or consider returning to prospecting in Montana. But I do still read lots of literature, and feel deprived if I don't get out in the country with some frequency. I am also extremely ambivalent about the institutional church. Too many clergy in one room make me sweat. When I was in middle school, after taking one of those vocational aptitude tests, I realized that I wanted to be a pastor. But there was one big obstacle to that dream: I was female. A young male intern in my home congregation reminded me that women could not be ordained because Jesus didn't have female apostles, and because Scripture says that women should be silent when in church. I had learned somewhere that the intern's ideas were sexist and seemed wrong. It was my mother who encouraged me to pursue my interests in theology and the church. In fact, I credit much of my understanding of gender roles to watching my parents share their life in equal ways: in doing housework, having careers, and spending lots of time with me. I remember my dad vacuuming, and when my mom was at work, he cooked. That usually meant a TV dinner of spaghetti and meatballs, a slice of white bread, and canned peas. But when I went to church with them, I remember my pastor, whose only vision of what women should do in the church was to teach Sunday school, sing in the choir, and bake pies for the winter fair. One year when the men on the church council decided to do something different with the monies raised by the women's baking, the women's group rebelled. They wore buttons with their motto: "Pie Power." They won. They received their monies to do with as they pleased. I still admire those women.

Later on in seminary I would encounter moments over and over again when being a female in a male profession was hazardous to one's health. I suppose that's why I am suspicious, and to some degree will always be ambivalent about going to church. Two years ago I filled in as the interim campus pastor while our pastor went on sabbatical to Africa. This was my first full-time position in which I would serve as a pastor. Along with the staff, I planned, led, and attended four worship services a week, which included a Wednesday and Sunday Eucharist. The year transformed me. I fell in love with the students and looked forward to worship. However, at the end of nine months, and after attending lots and lots of worship, I longed for a sabbatical, one in which I could recharge, work on my writing, and not attend so many services.

So, that year while I was on sabbatical, I attended services at Our Lady of Beaver Creek. About ten miles from Sioux Falls, Beaver Creek is a nature preserve and is under the care of the South Dakota State Park system. I drove there several times a week, taking my two large dogs with me. I know that road as well as I once knew the path up to Charlie's. I have also developed a very amateurish love of photography, and after several months I had a visual record of the weekly trips. The road dips and bends through pastures and large country homes, and finally turns into the nature preserve. Last year, in the late spring, the dogs discovered the joy of rolling in a dead deer carcass. This was followed by a romp through weeds and vines. Washing the stench out was going to take more than the cold-water shower Gary and I could give them at the water pump. So off we drove to the doggie wash, which is next to the car wash. In layer after layer, with lots of soap and warm water, and two baths, we stripped off the stench. They smelled better. Not great, but better. For weeks, which turned into a couple months, we had to avoid that section of the trail. We also avoid it during the height of tick season. I have watched the sun setting while hot-air balloons launch from one of the picnic sites, and I also have driven on icy stretches of packed snow while my dogs whine and croon with anticipation of running in fresh snow. It seems that if I don't get to Beaver Creek at least once or twice a week, I get edgy and out of sorts.

I'm a high-energy, high-maintenance, fairly competitive person, and so I must temper that side of myself with something to refresh it. Or I burn out, which I'm prone to do. And more often than not, I burn out and don't know it until something in my body quits, like my shoulders and hands that just give out from too much computer work. Trying meditation hasn't worked, and I hate yoga. But I've learned to like and maybe even love Pilates. It is not so meditative in nature. I have relearned how to breathe again. Funny thing—the way I learned to breathe as a young flute student is the same way I relearned to breathe now while doing Pilates. The breath is controlled from the diaphragm. I don't play the flute or piano much anymore. I worked too much at the computer with shoulders and hands in tense positions. I've been in physical therapy multiple times for repetitive stress injuries. I know that I need to listen and watch and rest. However, those things are not easy for me to do, and so sometimes I solicit help from the monks at St. John's Abbey and the nuns at St. Ben's Abbey.

My first sabbatical was up at St. John's at an ecumenical institute during the winter of 1997, quite memorable for its record breaking snows and floods. Some of my colleagues' homes were flooded in Grand Forks, North Dakota. Large sections of Fargo, North Dakota, and Moorhead, Minnesota, were under water. I traveled Highway 23, north and east, each week back up to the Abbey after a weekend at home with Gary. The sanctuary at St. John's Abbey and the apartments at the institute were designed by Marcel Brauer. In fact, the whole of St. John's reflects the Benedictine values of hospitality, work, prayer, and the simple, open architecture of Brauer. The new guesthouse, built just a few years ago, is stark, but beautiful in its simplicity and clean lines. My husband and I returned once from a weekend up at St. John's, vowing to rid our lives and house of clutter. We'll see about that. But spending three days with no distractions left us feeling quiet, at home in ourselves and with each other. We drove to St. Ben's on Sunday for Mass with the nuns. Maybe it's worshipping with mostly women, or the hospitality with which they offer the liturgy, or the stillness and light of the sanctuary, but every time I worship there, I end up in tears. I am not sure why, and I really don't want to figure it out. It's enough to be there. It helps me live through the next weeks and months. These nuns and monks, while tied deeply to the institutional church, are also a bit suspicious of it. In that way and in many others, I feel a kinship with them. Just to indicate either their great sense of humor, or a little liturgical equality, the nuns made sure that the presider's chair in the sanctuary is the same size as all the other seats. I've known some of the monks to quietly copreside with female clergy during the Eucharist (usually held in some basement). They welcome everyone to Mass, no questions asked. I always feel welcome. God's grace finds itself in the smiles of the nuns who are at the welcome center, in the light voices of the choir, and in the footsteps of the monks in the hallway.

The liturgy provides me with words and sounds when I don't have them. I also am joined to the whole company of saints, in words and prayers, throughout the centuries, said together in worship. I particularly love Compline, prayer at the close of the day: "The Lord Almighty grant us a quiet night and peace at the last." When thoughts race through my head and my shoulders ache with exhaustion from the day's stress, these words bring a sense of peace and hope. A quiet night. Peace at the last.

I have prayed these words at campus-ministry retreats, around the campfire during summer, and alone at night. And when the spoken and printed word exhausts me, I listen. Mostly to music. Lately, I have been listening again and again to music written and sung by Cyprian Consiglio. He often enlists John Pennington, a percussionist, to play along. Somewhere in the middle of chant and percussion I can let go. I love percussion. Maybe that's why I partially enjoyed being a piano major in college. I didn't want to play the timpani or wait for endless measures to pound the chimes. But I could play the piano, forcefully or quietly. I loved a piece by Alberto Ginastera that I memorized for a recital: a wild, South American piece that swept my fingers over the black keys with pounding rhythms. And I still like percussion in various forms—from the dance beat of hip hop to the pounding quad toms of a marching band drum line. In fact, I have told my husband that I really would like to have a marching band drum line at my memorial service, in honor of Martin Luther, who said that music was the resonant word of God and that faith was movement.

Faith is movement, adventure, and resonance. Whether in the orbits of the planets around the sun or in electrons of an atom, I believe that the creation of God, our cosmos, is charged with energy and vivacity. Despite starting in honors math and science courses in middle school and high school, I secretly preferred to study literature, music, and languages. However, in college, during a physics course about musical acoustics, I had what I could call my first musical-metaphysical encounter with God. Studying the harmonics of the overtone series brought together the physical nature of creation with the beauty of musical instruments and compositions. And then I applied what I had studied about musical acoustics as I practiced and played a Mozart flute concerto or a Bach three-part invention. Now in my middle years, for reasons I'm not sure of, I am fascinated by the sciences—especially the biological and medical sciences. I want to know more and more about this world in which I live and that I confess that God has created. I look forward to the science updates every Tuesday in the *New York Times*.

Sometimes what I learn about this world is beautiful, and other times it is frightening and awful. And of course, the natural world isn't really natural, if that means it's untainted by humankind. We have coevolved together, with and from the natural world. We are creatures. When I look at my two dogs, I see something of myself and of God in both of them. That's not some kind of sentimental statement about *God* and *dog*. I know better than that. I'm not innocent when it comes to my love of creatures. I have dogs as companion animals, eat steak once in a while, and wear leather shoes. I know that some of the medical procedures that have saved my life have probably required animals to sacrifice theirs. I'm not sure what to do with all this. This is a project and proposal for me to work on in the near future. I'm always amazed at how little those of us in the church pay attention to all of God's creatures. We are so concerned with our own personal life and faith that we ignore and forget about that garden of Eden from which we came, which was teeming with diverse wildlife and was full of plants, rivers, trees, and other creations of God. If there really is a new heaven and new earth, then the delight will be to share this new world with companion dogs, trout, chimpanzees, robots, fellow humans, lice, and trees.

I often listen to "Salvation Is Created," a choral version of Psalm 74:12[2]: "Yet God my King is from of old, working salvation in the earth." I have listened to the piece for years and never listened carefully to the words. But I have always loved the title. So recently I looked up the words and the passage of Scripture to which they refer. The lyrics include these words: "Salvation is created, in the midst of the earth." Peter Tschesnokoff, a Russian, composed the music in 1912. The chorale proclaims, through its musical tones and harmonies, that God saves us, not apart from our lives and bodies, but in the midst of our lives, on this earth, and in our body-selves. Salvation does not refer to some saccharine, celestial place. When I listen—really listen—to the music, I can hear its sorrowful

---

2 Tschesnokoff, "Salvation Is Created." On *What Child Is This?*

notes amid the joy. It is as if St. Paul had set these words from Romans 8 to music: "all of creation groans with eager longing." Music is theology. That's probably why I have stayed Lutheran.

Martin Luther, despite all his faults, proclaimed the incarnation, not only in his writing, but also through his music, his passion for life. The Lutheran heritage has not always honored these roots. We have intellectualized and personalized a message about God's grace coming in the person of Jesus Christ. That's why Psalm 74 is so important for me: salvation is in and through the material world of human body-selves. I teach Luther's theology in both its sixteenth-century confessional forms and its new incarnations. Women have been ordained for forty years, the Evangelical Lutheran Church in America (ELCA) just approved ordination for gays and lesbians who are living in committed partnerships, and Roman Catholics lifted the condemnation against Luther. I teach Lutheran theology on a college campus whose identity comes from the ELCA. About 50 percent of our students are Lutheran. About another 25 percent of the students are Roman Catholic. Many come from rural settings and small towns set on the upper Great Plains. They tend to be a hardy lot, hardworking, nonconfrontational, and thoughtful. They are very similar to the students with whom I first went to college at Concordia in Moorhead, Minnesota.

I admit that both going to college and now teaching in the upper Midwest has taken some adjustment. I grew up in a town that was not racially diverse, but it also did not share the same ethnic and religious homogeneity that so much of the upper-Midwest culture does. No doubt geography plays a part. Once you cross the Missouri River and head west, things get bigger. Farms turn to ranches. Cows don't gather in feedlots but spread out across the grasslands. And the farther west you travel, the less churched one is likely to be. My friends were mostly Christian: Lutheran, Catholic, Methodist, Presbyterian, Disciples of Christ. But no one denomination or tradition stood out above the others. So I don't always understand the students I teach, nor do I always appreciate their backgrounds. But I have grown to respect them. And even more important, I have grown to love them. I love teaching. It's who I am. I can think of nothing more delightful than an engaging conversation with students about theodicy or Luther's thoughts and rants about the sacraments. I love to watch the students come alive as the ideas roll around in their heads and off their lips. Everyone should study theology. I believe that one reason my marriage can be such fun is that we both love to teach;

Gary teaches band to elementary-school and middle-school students. Sometimes we find that middle-school kids are not so different from first-year college students. They can be awkward. They are enthusiastic, not yet so jaded by all the educational tasks piled on them. And they are unpredictable. But they are fun, and we love to both teach and learn from and with them.

And like the students, I long to go on journeys, to places that will challenge my narrow vision of where and how others in the world live. Recently a student of mine gave her senior sermon, about the places she has traveled during her four years at Augustana College, and how she has come to see all of them as home. Meredith Reynolds, along with the other students in the Augustana band, was in the middle of Egypt giving a concert when the revolution broke out in 2011. Instead of retreating into fear, she forged ahead and spoke with her Egyptian hosts. The foreign became familiar. She spoke so well about how travel has helped her to be at home:

> This is why we travel. Because in all, life isn't about politics, or about governments, or about religions or money. It's about friendship. It's about acceptance. It's about kindness and compassion and love. It's about people. Because for better or for worse, we're all still people. It's about turning off the TV and tearing down the walls. Keeping our eyes open to similarities, our minds open to differences, and our hearts open to each other. Understanding what you can, respecting what you can't, and letting every moment make you grow as a human being. In the end, we're not our governments or our religions or our bank statements. It's about going exploring, facing fear head on, and making home wherever you are.[3]

She reminded all of us that home is where we are, created from the relationships we have with one another.

Gary and I talk about where we'd like to retire. While we are still some years from that moment in our life, nonetheless, it is true that time goes faster as one ages. Sooner rather than later, we will be at another threshold in our life. How we choose to cross that threshold is yet another spiritual task we will face. One thing we know now for sure is that wherever we are, we will be with those who mean the most to us. As much as I'd love to move and live in the mountains, I will most likely live here on the prairie, to look out and know that my horizon is blessed with those who love me.

3. Reynolds, Senior Sermon, "You Transplanted a Vine from Egypt."

To Know Who We Are, We Must Know Where We Are

We learn most about who and whose we are when we discover where we are. Such learning comes through living fully and completely, immersed in the quotidian of our lives. God meets us where we are, and not only meets us, but makes a home with us and in us. Christians claim that God is incarnate in all creation, and in Jesus the Christ in a particular and powerful way. In the history of Christianity, the incarnation of God is often expressed as a tension between the universal and particular, the general and the specific. Is God more present in Jesus the Christ than in the whole of creation? Is God's power and presence more fully known in humans than in the other creatures? I find myself at home with those theologians throughout the tradition who claim that God's grace is first and most fully expressed for all creation, in, with, and under all things. This is the context from which I understand the specific and particular revelation of God in Jesus the Christ. I confess, first and foremost, that God is the Creator, and I believe that God's creation and redemption merge through the powerful love and grace that God has for all things. I repeat: *all things*. God dwells not only in humans but also in the cosmic home of all creation. The horizon of God's grace must be as wide as possible, and the scope of God's love as specific as each creature. In a world where so many people are homeless, and when we are destroying the habitats and homes of the creatures that surround us, we cannot afford to live out a gospel that is pinched, narrow, or exclusively our own. We must stand on the horizon, with arms wide open, to welcome the God who desires to make a home in each of us. Then and only then will we really stand and see the universal scope of God's love and grace.

2

The Spiritual Significance of Place

EXCURSUS

I HAVE NO IDEA WHERE *I am going. I am completely disoriented. Everything begins to look exactly the same. I turn one way, thinking that it must be the way home, and realize that I have gone the opposite direction. When I look out at the sky, all I see is the same horizontal plain, stretching ahead for endless miles. This was my first experience of trying to find my way around the roads of the upper Midwest. And to my embarrassment, after living here over twenty years, I can still get lost. Completely and totally disoriented. One of my greatest delights in the last two years is owning a vehicle that has a compass in it; now when I head out on the country roads, I can tell what direction I am going! Lest I think that I'm the only one for whom this experience of dislocation happens, I have commiserated with friends from other parts of the country, especially from the mountains, and they have the same experience of thinking they are headed the right way, only to find themselves miles in the other direction.*

Growing up in Montana, I learned to figure where I was going not by knowing directions as such, or looking at the placement of the sun (and that changes seasonally), but by knowing which mountain ranges to look for in which direction. Maybe I learned to find my way in this manner because that is how my father, who was an air-traffic controller, helped pilots when

The Spiritual Significance of Place

they were lost. He had to figure out which mountain ranges they were near, and help them find the airport. I knew that the Spanish Peaks were south, toward Yellowstone Park, and that the Bridger Mountains were north. East and West were marked by other distinct mountain peaks. To this day, when I have to figure out directions, I have to take the landscape of the Gallatin Valley and place it in my head so that I can orient myself. When I look at the endless Dakota horizons, still after all these years, I can become completely dislocated. When I am out for a drive in the country, for a brief moment, my stomach flutters, and I feel slightly dizzy. I will have no idea how to get home. Sometimes I have to stop and ask for directions. The usual response often goes like this: "Take this road a half mile north, and then turn west for two miles." That just makes me feel even more nervous because I don't want to admit to the person that I just asked for directions that I have no idea where north or west is. But if for one moment, I pause and take a breath, then I can relocate the map of my native Gallatin Valley in my head, and I try to place it on top of the geography in which I am lost. I might have a moment of luck and find my way home. In a sense, I live in two geographies, in two places at one time. The mountains of Montana and the plains of the Dakotas reside in me simultaneously. It's like living in a restless topography, and I have spent most of my life crossing from one to another. For me, life has been living on a perpetual border, between the places that orient my life.

The Importance of Place and How It Shapes Our Identity

Story, Location, Family, Identity

We connect with people in places and ways that we least expect. In the middle of the 1990s, I traveled to Germany for the first time. I was alone but armed with advice and directions from my friends. I had studied German in graduate school, but somehow the theological German that I had learned in ten weeks was no help when I tried to ask for directions to the train station. The more nervous I became, the worse my memory would become, and I could only remember theological words: *Gott* and *Rechtfertigung*. I was traveling from Potsdam to Wittenberg, and I had to change trains in some small little town. I boarded the first train, relieved to know I had at least started my journey in the right direction. When it came time to change trains, I stepped out of the car and onto a platform with a small ticket building. I walked into the building, and three people stared at me. Two men were sitting together: their shaved heads, nose

The Geography of God's Incarnation

rings, and tattoos were their dress code. Seated on the other side from them was another man who was quietly reading a book. Suddenly, when the two men began asking me questions in German, none of which I could understand, I broke out into a sweat and remarked that I didn't speak German. I felt vulnerable and very alone.

I'm not sure whether I spoke that in German or English, but then all three men were laughing. Finally the other, quiet man, looked up from his book, and said in English: "They think you are American and want to know what you think about Monica Lewinski and Bill Clinton." I broke into laughter and what followed was a conversation translated between me, the two German men, and the other quiet man, who turned out to be from Sudan. We exchanged pleasantries about German beer and American politics, and waited for the next train. When we boarded the next train, I sat with the man from Sudan, and in the course of a lengthy conversation he discovered that he might have relatives near Sioux Falls who had immigrated through Lutheran Social Services. All of a sudden, on a train ride in Germany, my world had become much smaller.

Place forms our human identity. From our cultural to our geographical landscapes, we know who we are by explaining where we are from. Our identity is linked to our location. Philip Sheldrake, an Anglican theologian, claims that place shapes our human identity through our memories, our bodies, and the stories that we tell. "The concept of place refers not simply to geographical location but to a dialectical relationship between environment and human narrative. Place is space that has the capacity to be remembered and to evoke what is most precious."[1] For many families, part of the fun of going on vacation involves telling stories again and again about what happened on that famous trip. As the details unfold, people will embellish, and immediately the trip becomes alive again. Sheldrake notes that places are embedded in our culture and contexts, which then are interpreted in their many layers. Places are like enculturated texts that require interpretation.[2]

Stories about places unfold through the ways they are told, and so both the stories and the places change through time. Our memories can be triggered by a certain smell or sound. In one of my favorite books, a mystery by Nevada Barr, the main character recalls her previous life as a camper and hiker on the trails. "Anna had reached an age where sleeping

---

1. Sheldrake, *Spaces for the Sacred*, 1.
2. Ibid, 3.

The Spiritual Significance of Place

on the ground with the bugs and the sticks no longer held the appeal it once had. Still, the smell of woodsmoke on a winter morning called for a strange nostalgia, an ache that vacillated between a yearning for home and hearth and a need to carve an adventure out of untrammeled land. Enjoying the sweet sting of this dichotomy, she buried her hands in the pockets of her parka and lengthened her stride."[3] Landscape is mediated through our memories of it, the way it smells, the sounds it makes, the way it feels on our fingertips. We remember things through the rituals we create with those memories: *Remember when*. Tales told around the campfire. Some people lose their memories or have no memories of a place. Some places carry mythic or epic qualities. Names are important to memory and to the stories we tell about the places. The names can come in layers, depending on who tells the stories and how they are remembered. For example, in South Dakota, sites will have both Native American names and names given by those who came later. The place where Mount Rushmore stands was named the Black Hills by Euro-Americans and is known as the Paha Sapa by the Lakota. Places reveal their meanings through the names and stories told about them.[4]

When I travel to the South Dakota Badlands, I notice that the layers of rock tell the stories of all who have inhabited this land of extremes. The Lakota peoples called this area *mako sica*, or "bad lands." French trappers, who came much later, also referred to these lands as bad areas that they dreaded traveling through.[5] About seventy five million years ago, a great sea covered much of the Great Plains. After the sea receded, when the Rocky Mountains formed, the area was exposed to the sun and air. The land is like a giant museum where exhibits of both the living and dead are on display for me to see. Layers of fossils, of the extinct creatures that once inhabited this land, have been revealed, and they tell us much about what the area must have been like around twenty-five to thirty-five million years ago. When we have traveled during the offseason, when the tourists are few, I can see more closely what the Badlands tell me. These spires of rock and sediment exemplify what Philip Sheldrake says about places as texts. And when I think that I have begun to understand what is in those layers and what it might mean to me, I know there is always more beneath. "Every place has an excess

---

3. Barr, *High Country*, 58.
4. Sheldrake, *Spaces for the Sacred*, 17.
5. Ibid.

of meaning beyond what can be seen or understood at any one time."[6] That's why I love to return. I always discover something new in those strangely shaped deposits of red, brown, yellow, and black. Thousands of years from now the South Dakota Badlands will recede again. My hope is that the ways humans remember these great bands of colored rock will tell us something powerful not only about the rocks but also about the ways that we cared for and loved these Badlands.

Our ancestry is cut and shaped through the places we inherit. Many people in the United States make a kind of pilgrimage back to the lands of their ancestors, to see up close where they are from. My Lutheran ancestors migrated to different parts of the United States and came with very different agendas. In the part of the upper Midwest, where I live now, Norwegians came with a piety that was the opposite of its institutional mother church. Hans Nielsen Hauge rejected the formality and apathy of Norway's institutional church, and he reemphasized Luther's understanding of the priesthood of all believers. This democratic version of Lutheranism spread throughout much of the upper Midwest Lutheranism, and with it a rejection of anything that smelled, looked like, or felt like the old church in Norway, or worst yet, of anything papal.[7] And the distance between parishes meant that clergy couldn't reach all the parishes every week. For many local congregations, members received the sacraments of baptism and communion a few times a year when the pastor could come. When I asked local Lutheran congregants why they hadn't always had weekly Eucharist, they replied that it had always been that way. Upon further reflection, they seemed to think it had something to do with not "looking too Catholic," and with how frequently the pastors had been able to come to congregations when the parishes of the prairies first started. No doubt both sentiments came together in their sacramental practices. The doctrines often arise out of practices (*lex orandi, lex credendi*). I think that the wide-open prairie expanses have shaped the local Lutheran doctrine in more ways than we realize.

Religion is not the only force that shapes the practices of a place. Even science and medicine are influenced heavily by how disease and health are understood and studied. We are learning more and more about how much infectious disease is influenced by how humans interact with nature.[8] Medical geography is a relatively new discipline that examines

---

6. Ibid.
7. "Record Group 4."
8. Robbins, "The Ecology of Disease."

how geography shapes the spread and understanding of disease. Other scientists are studying the ecology of a disease:

> Teams of veterinarians and conservation biologists are in the midst of a global effort with medical doctors and epidemiologists to understand the 'ecology of disease.' It is part of a project called Predict, which is financed by the United States Agency for International Development. Experts are trying to figure out, based on how people alter the landscape, with a new farm or road, for example, where the next diseases are likely to spill over into humans and how to spot them when they do emerge, before they can spread.[9]

These are reminders of how nature, landscape, and humans are so intricately connected. So often we approach the landscape as a kind of container we fill instead of the matrix of relationships in which we are grounded. Like religion and its rituals, science and its practices are embedded in their local landscapes.

Several recent books about the topography of illness reconnect landscape, family, genetics, and medical science. For example, Masha Gessen in her work called *Blood Matters* explains the evolutionary links between cancer, family, and her spiritual origins. Our genetic inheritance establishes itself in the landscape of our ancestry. Gessen carries a genetic mutation that "kills women early, earlier and earlier with each generation, through breast and ovarian cancer."[10] Genetics are passed on through common blood from common ancestors and are often traced geographically, to the place of origins. Gessen explains: "We have common blood. The mutation I carry is called a 'founder mutation,' which means it goes back to a single event: one person who was born with a mutant gene and passed it on to his or her offspring, who passed it on and on."[11] Her genetically mutant gene goes beyond the split that occurred with the Ashkenazim and Sephardim. Blood, religion, and ancestry link to geography. The incarnation of a disease is traceable not only through the blood of human bodies but also through the blood of the land in which these bodies were born and migrated. What Gessen realizes about her genetic ancestry goes to the root of what it means to be human: "I was transported to a new era, a future that will rest on a different understand-

9. Ibid.
10. Gessen, 7.
11. Ibid., 9.

ing not only of what causes things to go wrong in human beings, but of what makes a human being in the first place, and what connects any one of us to any other."[12] The maps through the human genome chart the landscape of our ancestral past and our postmodern future. This is also true for the way we inherit spiritual traditions. The way that religions have spread and migrated across territories shape the ways the religion itself is embodied and passed on from one generation to another.

Terry Tempest Williams in *Refuge: An Unnatural History of Family and Place* tells a story about memory, ancestry, her Mormon religion, and the landscape.[13] Like Gessen, Williams belongs to a family in which two women die from cancer too early in their lives. What she discovers is that exposure to the radiation from nuclear testing in the desert of Utah and Nevada during the 1940s and 1950s predisposed those in her family to cancer. When she finds out that she is losing her mother to ovarian cancer, she simultaneously chronicles her own loss and the loss of wildlife in the local bird refuge near where she lives. Both losses are linked to the ways humans wreak havoc on their environment without any thought about the cost of life. *Refuge* has become a classic text not only about death and dying, but also about how hope emerges from the protests that we make against the senseless loss of life. Toward the end of the book, Williams joins the protests of others at a nuclear site. The hope that Williams offers rests in the connections she creates between what others have considered and rendered separate. By telling her story, she connects her story to all other stories. I found myself in her place, in the connections she creates with her forebears and the topography of her daily life. When we tell the stories that create connections, we can link ourselves to others in our experiences of life and death, joy and sorrow, loss and connection. For those of us who can feel so disconnected in our daily lives, from family and friends, from our origins, from our spiritual values, telling our stories helps us to restore the connections that make us whole.

A more recent book, *The Wandering Gene and the Indian Princess*, is an account of how a young woman gets breast cancer. But it is much more than this. The story tells how "the gene gets in with her, the gene that has followed her from Judea to Sepharad to Mexico and up the winding aisle of

---

12. Ibid., 14.
13. Williams, *Refuge*, xx.

the Rio Grande."[14] Shonnie Median, a young Hispanc woman, inherits the BRCA1.185delAG, a gene that suppresses tumor growth, and so she dies of breast cancer. Along the path through her illness she discovers that she is not only from Native American roots and Spanish Catholics, but also from Sephardic Jews. This genetic mutation that she inherits comes from her latent Jewish ancestry. The story, told by Jeffrey Wheelright, connects religion, geography, and biological ancestry together in a spiritual quest about the disease of breast cancer. Wheelright provides a hermeneutics of disease through the lens of religion and place. This story reflects many of the same connections in Williams's *Refuge*: DNA is inherited through the blood of bodies and the soil of their origins. Landscape shapes our genetic makeup.[15] Wheelright writes: "In this depiction of the nature-nurture question, the landscape informs the life, and simultaneous other lives are implicit in the roads not taken, in the environments where life did not happen to take root."[16] The landscape itself creates the paths that genes take or ignore. This story's hermeneutic is one of connections or ligatures, between the landscape and DNA, religion and culture, the past and present. If we ignore the connections through which disease comes into the world, we cannot adequately treat or offer help to those who suffer from it. For example, the contemporary metaphor of "winning the war" on cancer ignores the way that cancer comes about in the first place. Evidently, disease is all of the above: genetic, environmental, spiritual, familial, and cultural. Terry Tempest Williams confirms this view when she says that an individual doesn't get a disease, a family does.

Williams cannot prove without a doubt that the women in her family get cancer from the nuclear fallout in Utah. But she does know that her father's memory was correct: "The September blast we drove through in 1957 was part of Operation Plumbbob, one of the most intensive series of bomb tests to be initiated. The flash of light in the night in the desert, which I had always thought was a dream, developed into a family nightmare. It took fourteen years, from 1957 to 1971, for cancer to manifest in my mother, the same time Howard L. Andrews, an authority in radioactive fallout at the National Institutes of Health, says radiation cancer requires to become evident."[17] Her memory, especially

---

14. Wheelwright, *The Wandering Gene*, 6.
15. Ibid.
16. Ibid.
17. Williams, *Refuge*, 20.

as she recalls her father's comments from that night, become re-membered in her acts of protest at the nuclear site. At the Last Supper, when Jesus says, "Do this in remembrance of me," he is not asking us to recall with fondness a nice meal that he had with his friends, but instead we are asked to remember and to recall. We are to bring to mind again and again those who suffer, so that we might be faithful to our calling to help those who are in need. Remembering is about restoring, rebuilding, and renewing the land and those who live in it. Remembering can be a faithful act of defiance against the ways we forget our place in the world. Our Christian faith *should* help us, not hinder us, in these faithful acts of remembrance. Williams writes, "What I do know, however, is that as a Morman woman of the fifth generation of Latter-Day Saints, I must question everything, even if it means losing my faith, even if it means becoming a member of a border tribe among my own people. Tolerating blind obedience in the name of patriotism or religion ultimately takes our lives."[18] When we become a member of the border tribe among our own people, we will gain a different perspective on our place. For Williams, and for me, religion is not about practicing allegiance to a set of beliefs or following a leader blindly, but instead it is about living out the gift of God's gracious love on behalf of the neighbor who is nearby or far away. Whether it is the person next door or in another country, millions today are experiencing a crisis of place, of being dislocated. The place that is most threatened is our planet earth.

Crisis of Place

Excursus #2: A Confession about Our Place in the World

1. *We turn some places into idols, claiming that they are our gods, leaving no room for the grace of God.*
2. *We push people out of their place. Some have been displaced through acts of genocide or by a simple erasure of their place from the map.*
3. *We confine people to locations, limiting their mobility.*
4. *We neglect the environment around us, ignoring the ecology of who we are.*

---

18. Ibid., 286.

5. *We objectify those whom we consider others and put them in their places. For example, women and nature have been objectified, raped, and displaced for thousands of years.*
6. *We fear leaving somewhere and never venture into the larger world that God has created.*
7. *We ignore the present plights of earth by trying to return to some primeval pristine place, like a garden of Eden. We long for the good old days.*
8. *We ignore our present plight of place by trying to get to heaven, which we figure is our true spiritual home.*
9. *We disconnect the land from our bodies, ignoring that who we are is where we are.*
10. *And God's absolution to us: "The Word became flesh and made His home among us."*[19]

We humans, with our ever-expanding arsenals, have the power to completely destroy the place in which we all dwell—Earth. While some decry the affects of global warming as mere political rhetoric, others, including myself, are frightened and deeply concerned. If these warnings about how we can destroy the world ring true, then surely Christian theology must pay attention—now, before it is too late. Place is ultimately about our relationships—with everyone, and especially with God. And if we destroy our place, our home, then we can destroy our relationships with everyone.

Many cultural critics claim that the world is in a crisis of place. Borders, boundaries, and politics shape who is in and who is out of the world's power games. Philip Sheldrake rightly notes that the world is in a crisis of place, though the crisis happens in different ways depending on one's location. In the West, the crisis manifests as a "sense of rootlessness, dislocation or displacement."[20] We shape our world as we find our place within it, and this involves processes, people, and power dynamics. Contemporary theorists who work with the politics of place refer to these relationships as "geographies of struggle and resistance."[21] No one place has a single meaning. People interpret places differently. While that may

---

19. John 1:14, Common English Bible.
20. Sheldrake, *Landscapes of the Sacred*, 2.
21. Ibid., 5.

be obvious, it needs to be formally recognized in order to understand the power of place. We can wipe out the identity of someone or somewhere by simply removing them from a map.

On a recent report from National Public Radio, I learned that Juarez, Mexico, had been removed from the map. Their identity as a city was wiped out by people in El Paso, Texas, who were making the maps for tourists to that region. Marianne McCune reports on the perceptions of the people on the borderline between these two countries. The mayor of Juarez struggles with the perceptions about his city: corruption, violence, and drug cartels. So the United States government issued warnings for those Americans traveling to Juarez. Across the border, El Paso, Texas, is viewed as the safest city in the United States to which tourists might travel. But the cities and the mayors are inextricably linked through their related economies. They rely on each other. However, the mayor of El Paso discouraged people from crossing the border into Juarez because of the violence, and so when the maps were made for tourists, the city of Juarez was left off the map. In 2010, the news reported that Juarez "was removed off the map."[22] The man who makes the map explains that families have relatives in both cities; the borderline crosses family bloodlines. At the time of this writing, the maps are being drawn again, and this time by people in the city of Juarez and they are putting their city back on their own tourists' maps. They refuse to have their identity wiped out by others. Children in Juarez are repainting the bridges with art, trying to announce that their city is not unsafe for tourists. The way the maps are drawn by both cities shapes who benefits from the tourist economies. But both cities and peoples are trying to figure out how to remain visible even if the other renders them invisible, off the map.

When we are displaced, the relationships that connect and make us whole are broken and disconnected. Being displaced is like being disconnected. A year ago, my husband went on a bike trek across Wisconsin with his brother. Years ago when we didn't have cell phones, I might have received a call once or twice from him along the way, letting me know that he was all right. However, now, when the phone rings, and I answer it and hear my husband's voice, I not only know that he is okay, but in a sense I know where he is. If I wanted to do it, I could track his GPS signal and follow the route of his bike trip. For all their hassles, I love cell phones. I feel connected to Gary in ways I never would have been, and we

---

22. McClune, "Rehabilitating Juarez's International Image."

enjoy sending our little texts and pictures, and receiving the occasional calls while he is on the way. I have plotted their course with MapQuest and have pictures from his iPhone so that I have a sense of where they are. We are connected, and the world feels right.

But I've had the other kind of phone calls. Sometimes they happen in the middle of the night. Many years ago, when we were first married, the phone would ring, often around 2:00 a.m. We would be in a deep sleep, and then suddenly, came the piercing sound of the phone. I would run to it, pick it up, and hear nothing. The line had gone dead; the person hung up. Disconnected. Oddly enough, I also felt displaced. I would try to go back to sleep, but the darkness which had once felt comfortable and had helped me go to sleep, now felt like the land of nightmares, and I felt haunted by it. Finally, the calls ended after three or four nights. We never did know who was calling or why. But I haven't forgotten that feeling of being wakened in the night and the sense of security shattered by the darkness and disconnection with the unnamed party.

For many people in the world, the feelings of disconnection and displacement are not the result of unanswered phone calls, but the reality of their daily lives. Millions of people are forced from their homelands and live permanently as refugees and immigrants. Emergencies create situations in which people must leave their homes: an earthquake destroys a city, civil war breaks out in a country, a tornado flattens farms and small towns, and drought kills crops and brings famine. These are the drastic and dramatic events that force people to flee and to find a livelihood elsewhere. Some people will eventually return and rebuild, while others can never go back. But for all, disconnection and disruption become the norm in their life.

In his widely read book, *The World Is Flat: A Brief History of the Twenty-First Century*, Thomas Friedman views the world as a landscape in which the power dynamics between corporations, countries, and communities have become more equal, creating a more level playing field in the world's business.[23] The old boundaries that once shaped the world's economies have eroded and exploded. This flattening out of the world's boundaries is altering the global scene. However, Harm De Blij, a Dutch geographer, challenges Thomas Friedman's notion that the world has become flat, that we are so mobile and free that we can move any place at any time. While the upwardly mobiles of the world might be able

---

23. Friedman, *The World Is Flat*, 2.

The Geography of God's Incarnation

to do that, the forces of place also limit the lives of millions of people. The confinement is frequently superimposed by the power and prestige of others who don't live in the places of confinement. To use a crude if disturbing analogy, I cringe every time I drive up to the massive cattle and hog confinement pens, where hundreds of animals spend their lives penned for the massive appetites of omnivores like myself. In some ways that are not so dissimilar, the economic appetites of those of us from the flat or mobile world are starving millions of people who are confined by their location. Contrary to its flat image, the earth, Blij says, is "physically as well as culturally, still very rough terrain, and in crucial ways its regional compartments continue to trap billions in circumstances that spell disadvantage."[24]

People who have the power and mobility move away from those who they find dispensable. When I grew up, I knew which side of the town the rich and highly educated people lived and the side of the town in which the "others" lived. I was right on the border between. People can be trapped in a place not only by poverty, but also by fears which immobilize them. If we have been taught to fear those who are other, then the best way to perpetuate the fear and security we want is to build walls, physically or metaphorically. It all depends where you are, on which side of the wall or fence you see the others across from you. Think of the notorious borders between us and them: the Berlin Wall, the Great Wall of China, Hadrian's Wall, U.S.–Mexican Border, and the walls of Jericho. Some borders are less obvious: the neighbor's fence, which side of town you live on, which pew you occupy in church, the space you leave between you and your family.

One of the strangest stories in all of scriptures about boundaries and the enemy is told in the book of Jonah. All the discussions about whether it is "real" or not or whether it pre-figures Jesus' death and resurrection are missing the point for me. I understand this story to be about God's call to Jonah to cross a boundary into enemy territory and Jonah is adamant he doesn't want to go. What Israelite would want to go to Nineveh? This capital of Assyria symbolized the hated enemy of Israel; the Assyrians had brutally killed thousands of Israelites, sent others into exile, and conquered their country. They were not just an other to Jonah: they were the enemy. Not only does Jonah not want to heed God's call, but he runs off to the end of the earth, to Tarshish, to flee from God's presence. He

---

24. De Blij, *The Power of Place*, ix-x.

The Spiritual Significance of Place

is angry about being sent into enemy territory. I won't repeat the most famous details of the story, but Jonah goes to Nineveh, everyone repents, God spares Nineveh, and Jonah broods underneath a plant and argues with God. End of story. From reading many Christian interpretations, I came to the conclusion that the reason Jonah didn't want to follow God's will is that he was really afraid that God would be merciful to the Ninevites. This is a story about how great God's inclusive mercy is and a lesson for Jonah to learn about that mercy. God loves even the enemy. Given that I am a Christian theologian, that has been my take on the story.

What if I weren't Christian, but Jewish? How would I hear the story of Jonah? And what if I was more sympathetic to the plight of Israel, who had suffered greatly at the hand of their oppressors? I've had an experience, which has at least offered a different reading of the Jonah text to me. One night in a class of mine I invited a Hebrew teacher and scholar, Professor Jill Storm, to come and give a lecture on the book of Jonah. She is also Jewish. Partway through her lecture I realized that I was getting uncomfortable and frustrated. She was hearing and noticing many different things in the story and they were challenging much of what I had learned about my own Christian interpretation. I realized that my own Christian bias was not letting me into the world where she stood from the perspective of her Jewish faith. We were on a border, between Christian and Jew, learning to think about God's relation to the enemy. I realized once again how my own Christian location in the world had kept me from crossing a border into another's religious territory. I know that for centuries Christians have not listened to Jews, who they have considered other (at best) and enemy (at worst). So, I know I needed to listen. And since her lecture, I have read more. I have read more Jewish interpretations, feminist interpretations, and postcolonial ones.[25] I have discovered the multiple ways that different people read this story, and now I can let those multiple interpretations help me to expand and open my own crossing into the territories of those to whom I must listen.

Professor Storm's Jonah was ultimately more interesting to me than the one I had constructed. She remarked, "Jonah was an Israelite. The people of Nineveh were not Israelites. They were Others. They were foreigners. They were heathens."[26] And they weren't just any heathens; they were people who had desecrated the Jews. Some Jewish interpret-

---

25. Ryu, "Silence as Resistance," 195–218.
26. Storm, "Caring, Context and Otherness."

29

ers suggest that they were the Nazis of their day. So, then, how does my interpretation stand up from this side of the story, that of the Jews who have suffered for millennia under the oppressors? Professor Storm compared a Christian and a Jewish perspective: "For Christians this is a story about caring for the Other, yes, but it is also about grace . . . about being forgiven, and being forgiven without having to do anything to receive it. This word DO is important. But Jonah is Jewish, and according to Jewish tradition, forgiveness requires repentance and repentance requires not just saying one is sorry or sitting among the ashes, but actually requires turning around and *doing* things differently. Turning around and *living* differently."[27] As a Lutheran who has been trained to learn that "doing" anything is an act of the "law," I can see how I interpreted the Jonah text as I have. But something about her perspective also resonated with mine. I have worked for years with victims of sexual abuse and know that forgiveness is a tough issue for the victims. Does forgiveness mean simply forgetting? Or excusing the abuse? Or does forgiveness also require repentance by the victimizer? When I get inside this scenario of sexual abuse, all of a sudden, the perspective of Professor Storm makes all the difference in the world to me.

Like Jonah, those who have been abused would be frustrated if the abuser only goes through the outward signs of repentance but doesn't turn their lives around and change. Storm noted, "But the Ninevites only go through the motions and rituals of repentance; they don't actually change their lives. This would have frustrated Jonah. To the readers of this story, it may seem the Ninevites were the Others, that it's the Ninevites who need to be cared for, loved, and honored. But remember, Jonah, Yonah, was Jewish. To the Assyrians, the Ninevites, to whom Jonah was sent to prophesy, Jonah was actually the Other. The Ninevites decimated Israel, destroying the northern tribes, destroying Jonah's people. That changes things a bit, yes?"[28] Yes, indeed. A great deal changes. All of a sudden, the story changes for me. Jonah is angry at this God who is supposed to have mercy upon and take care of those who have been victims, particularly for Israel. To Jonah, the repentance of Nineveh appears to lack specific action and change, and so he questions God's judgment, in more ways than the obvious. Who is this God? Jonah isn't sure any longer that he can trust either the mercy or the judgment of God. The borders in

27. Ibid.
28. Ibid.

The Spiritual Significance of Place

this text determine its interpretation—whether the border rests between Israel and Assyria, colonized and colonizers, faithful and unfaithful, God and prophets, Christians and Jews. As in most stories from Scripture, the truth does not come from just one perspective here but from many. What I have learned again is that for all the talk about loving the enemy, it is damned hard to do. And we need to have permission to question God amid it all.

In a more contemporary mode, I read echoes of the Jonah tale into the story about Dietrich Bonhoeffer, a twentieth-century Lutheran theologian. Furious at the way the churches were reacting to the extermination and slaughter of the Jews, Bonhoeffer joined the underground plot to assassinate Hitler. Of course, what is ironic about this choice was that he had tried to remain a pacifist. He had always claimed that violence was *not* the way to deal with the enemy. Through his early years as a pastor and professor, he spoke out about the Jewish atrocities and also realized that his decision to join the resistance movement put his own life in danger.

While Bonhoeffer was ultimately faithful to his vocation of helping the Jews and resisting Hitler, he had moments of doubt and reluctance to follow God's call. In 1930 and 1931, Bonhoeffer studied at Union Theological Seminary in New York where he encountered the theology and ethics of Reinhold Neibuhr and also worked at a church in Harlem. He was saddened at the racism in America and made analogies to the Nazi treatment of the Jews. He went back to Germany and stayed for several more years; but in 1939, a few months after the horrors of Kristallnacht, Dietrich Bonhoeffer was invited once again to come to Union Seminary where he could have safe harbor. He left on a ship bound for America. Almost immediately after leaving Germany, Bonhoeffer realized that he had made a mistake, and when he arrived in America, he booked passage on the last steamer to leave American soil and cross the Atlantic.

He knew that he could not speak for his native land if he didn't return to it. He wrote to Reinhold Neibuhr in 1939: "I shall have no right to participate in the reconstruction of Christian life in Germany after the war if I do not share the trials of this time with my people . . . Christians in Germany will face the terrible alternative of either willing the defeat of their nation in order that Christian civilization may survive, or willing the victory of their nation and thereby destroying our civilization. I know which of these alternatives I must choose; but I cannot make this choice

31

in security."²⁹ Bonhoeffer's call was tied to a country, and when he chose to flee that place, he would no longer have been effective in carrying out his vocation. When he returned to Germany from the United States, he continued to experience the harassment of the Gestapo, was forced to stop preaching and publishing, and was eventually killed by the Nazis.

For Bonhoeffer, Christ was the center of all things. To follow Christ would mean taking a journey into the midst of life's pain and suffering. Bonhoeffer's call to a place involved a vocation of loving and serving the neighbor, even the enemy. In this enemy love we find the chief parallel between the Jonah story and Bonhoeffer's biography. While most of us are not the likes of Jonah or Bonhoeffer, we are called by God to be in specific places to fulfill our vocation: maybe in the hospital as a nurse to work with those who are dying, or to teach in the public schools, or to be a barista at the local coffee shop. But in each of our own situations, we are tempted to leave the place to which we are called and to flee from our obligations of caring for the neighbor. We are most alive in the places that God calls us to serve the world. Neighbor love and being alive go hand in hand with remaining in the place where God calls us to be. When we stand at the threshold, crossing between borderlands, we are both at home in God and open to our neighbor, even to our enemy.

---

29. Quoted in Metaxas, *Bonhoeffer*, 321.

3

An Incarnational Methodology
How We Notice Where We Are

EXCURSUS

Looking Intently

WE ARE ALL LEARNING *to see again, learning to see intently. I have always found this little passage in the Gospel of Mark to be a strange one (thanks in great part to the in-sights of Dr. Richard Bowman). From Mark 8:22–26, we read: "They came to Bethsaida. Some people brought a blind man to him and begged him to touch him. He took the blind man by the hand and led him out of the village; and when he had put saliva on his eyes and laid his hands on him, he asked him, 'Can you see anything?' And the man looked up and said, 'I can see people, but they look like trees, walking.' Then Jesus laid his hands on his eyes again; and he looked intently and his sight was restored, and he saw everything clearly. Then he sent him away to his home, saying, 'Do not even go into the village.'"*

I have questions. Why does Jesus take the man out of the village? Why does Jesus have to touch the man again, without the saliva? This time the man looks intently, and his sight is restored. Is it restored because he looked intently? Didn't Jesus get it right the first time? The text doesn't really say. With what kind of eyes do we see the world around us? On one hand, we are blind to that which is around us. On the other hand, we see, but not very clearly. Then we let Jesus touch us again, and we see everything clearly. But notice the words: we must first look intently, and then our sight is restored; that is, we can see everything clearly. We must look intently—closely, fixedly, carefully, attentively, keenly, and absorbedly. That's what the thesaurus on my computer says. Eugene Peterson, in his own translation of this Markan passage, uses different words to describe the restored vision of the blind man: "The man looked hard and realized that he had recovered perfect sight, saw everything in bright, twenty-twenty focus" (The Message). *To look intently is to have bright, twenty-twenty focus.*

I'm learning to see my place within creation, and I feel much like the blind man. I really don't know how to look. So, I'm practicing by watching the artwork of Sheila unfold in its magnificence each week. The details on the paintings reveal vibrant colors, subtle textures, and different patterns. Slowly, I'm observing them and also taking in what difference my changing observations make to my interpretation and view of the artwork. But that's not enough. I'm also discerning what is happening in the landscape of my own life. For example, I'm much more attentive in spring to the variant greens that are popping up, to the pregnant buds, to the variegated grasses in my yard, to the soybeans planted row by row, and to foliage of the distant hills as they wake up from slumber under wet and heavy snows. Green is not just a color. It's a way of seeing the world.

I sat with my mother-in-law yesterday while we waited in the doctor's office for her husband to finish with his appointment. We talked about her eyesight and how it's failing. She has macular degeneration and is the opposite of the sightless man. She used to see things in bright, twenty-twenty focus. Now it's as if she sees people, but they are like trees walking. They are vague, moving shapes. She knows there is a television on the wall but has no idea what pictures are flashing on the screen. Her eyesight will only be worse as she ages. However, I've noted something else about her that is getting better. She is noticing the little things in life as she hears them and attends to them. She listens intently, with a kind of aural twenty-twenty focus. She is grateful for every conversation, for time to just sit and visit. This summer her grandson will get married, and she will get to be there, maybe not with twenty-twenty eyesight but surely with an open and compassionate heart. She listens intently, perceives deeply, and responds with grace. Carol is learning to see the world with her heart, and I will learn from her. I need to learn how to see, not only with my eyes, but with my heart. I am learning from Carol. I will learn from someone else.

An Incarnational Methodology

I was on sabbatical. People would ask me, "Where have you been? Have you been anywhere exciting" (usually meaning somewhere overseas)? I answer: "I've been going to the same places, again and again, usually accompanied by Byron and Jack, my two large dogs." I realized that I needed to put into words what I was learning about where I was going and where I've been. I am trained as an academic, and I write about what I know. But this habitual way of doing that was failing. Stuck in the middle of finishing one book manuscript and trying to start writing another, I realized that words weren't working. I am also trained as a musician; I hear things. And my husband says I have an acute sense of smell. But I knew that I needed to find other ways to help me and others experience the places I've been and will go. I needed to expand my sensory vocabulary! So, without intention of doing so, I embarked on a pilgrimage of learning to see.

Almost every day the dogs leapt into the Honda CR-V and we headed east toward Beaver Creek Nature Preserve and then to Sheila's house nearby. I walked up the stairs to her art studio. Over the weeks that followed, I watched her gallery of paintings transform from vague forms of shadow, color, and light into landscapes that told a story. When Sheila tells a story, she does so with a paintbrush. And I watched the narratives unfold stroke by stroke, as colors changed and the viewpoint shifted. She was teaching me to think with my eyes.[1] So instead of traveling to far-off places, I stayed close by and began to watch an artist. She taught me that I could simply go to nearby places and learn to picture them with new eyes. So sight became a new portal for all the senses: for thinking incarnationally. What I discovered is that as I learned to see anew, all my other senses were intensified. I started noticing the different birdcalls, paying attention to the word choices I made, and feeling the soft, curly fur on my dogs. The senses are a form of thinking, of receiving the world through our bodies. And now I was learning through a new incarnational methodology by practicing careful observations, taking notice of details, and catching a glimpse of something I had previously ignored. Many passages in Scripture attest to our need to see, to touch, and to know.

Jesus healed the blind and welcomed those whose faith needed confirmation through sight. For me, Thomas, the disciple of Jesus who is

---

1. "My earlier work had taught me that artistic activity is a form of reasoning, in which perceiving and thinking are indivisibly intertwined. A person who paints, writes, composes, dances, I felt compelled to say, thinks with his sense" (Arnheim, *Visual Thinking*, v).

The Geography of God's Incarnation

called the doubter, might be the patron saint of sight, and thus of faith. From the twentieth chapter of the Gospel according St. John:

> *24 Thomas, the one called Didymus, one of the Twelve, wasn't with the disciples when Jesus came. 25 The other disciples told him, "We've seen the Lord!"*
>
> *But he replied, "Unless I see the nail marks in his hands, put my finger in the wounds left by the nails, and put my hand into his side, I won't believe."*
>
> *26 After eight days his disciples were again in a house and Thomas was with them. Even though the doors were locked, Jesus entered and stood among them. He said, "Peace be with you." 27 Then he said to Thomas, "Put your finger here. Look at my hands. Put your hand into my side. No more disbelief. Believe!"*
>
> *28 Thomas responded to Jesus, "My Lord and my God!"*
>
> *29 Jesus replied, "Do you believe because you see me? Happy are those who don't see and yet believe."*
>
> *30 Then Jesus did many other miraculous signs in his disciples' presence, signs that aren't recorded in this scroll. 31 But these things are written so that you will believe that Jesus is the Christ, God's Son, and that believing, you will have life in his name."*[2]

Faith helps us to see; it is a gift from God. It reminds me of what Nikos Kazantzakis wrote: "Within me even the most metaphysical problem takes on a warm physical body which smells of sea, soil, and human sweat. The word in order to touch me must become warm flesh, only then do I understand, when I can smell, see, and touch."[3] And the way I learned to see where I was going required that I open my eyes and notice. I needed to pay attention, to pause and look intently. And so I'll tell you something about where I went while on sabbatical.

Where have I been? I learned that I didn't need to go to Oz to find out that home is right where I am. When I went to Sheila's studio week after week, I recognized that her paintings had changed again and again. The landscape looked warmer, the buildings cooler. The season had turned from spring to fall. Smaller strokes replaced large swaths of color, filling in the canvas with new details. Textures appeared where they weren't

---

2. John 20:24–31 (CEB).

3. From Nicos Kazantzakas, *Report to Greco*, 43; quoted in Pederson, "Soteriological Motifs in the Theologies of Kazantzaki's and Luther," 96.

before. The light in the studio was different. What amazed me (and maybe Sheila) was that I noticed these changes. I have not considered myself to be a visually aware person. I know places more by sounds and smells, not by sight as such. And I rarely pay attention to lots of details. Now, I'm noticing. I'm not sure why. But being attentive to the fine points of Sheila's paintings has helped me to recognize the changing and subtle particulars in the landscapes of my daily, mundane life. Instead of viewing myself as simply a headshot, a visual symbol of my academically disembodied self, I began to see myself as a character within my own narrative landscape. So, now the days seem richer, and longer. They don't just pass by without my noticing. I am painfully aware that I am now into the middle years of my life, and some days have passed by without me becoming aware of the changes. By returning to the artwork of Sheila's and the landscape of Beaver Creek Nature Preserve, I am learning to go on a different type of pilgrimage. In musical language, I am experiencing exposition, development, and recapitulation. Home, away, and home again: all in a day's ride to an art studio and local nature preserve.

It's not that I have new glasses, although with aging eyes, a change in corrective eyewear is always helpful. No, I had to learn to see anew, again, with different eyes. And I did so unexpectedly.[4] And it's been because of my friendship with Sheila. She has given me new eyes. Learning to see is about the relationships we have with one another. "More generally, to see means to see in relation; and the relations actually encountered in percepts are not simple."[5] Over coffee shared during the many visits together, Sheila and I conversed about how we know and express that insight about the world around us. With Sheila's paintings and my words, we decided to collaborate on a way to show others how much we love the landscape around us. Uncertain about what would result from the process of this collaboration, we let time help us unfold the process in fits and starts. The result of this partnership was an exhibit at the Center for Western Studies at Augustana College during the fall of 2011 and early winter of 2012. We titled the show *Crossing Thresholds: Paintings and Prose*. The following notice advertised the exhibit:

> Where are we? The exhibit is a response to this question by an artist, Sheila Agee, and a writer, Ann Pederson. This exhibition is intended to be a window for reflection on our place in the

---

4. De Waal, *To Pause at the Threshold*, 9.
5. Arnhein, *Visual Thinking*. 54.

world. Places are like icons—the spiritual windows from which God looks into our world. Art is like that as well—revelations of the places we inhabit. During the development of this project, the artists felt like they were on a treasure hunt or a backpack. They wandered through the places Sheila has painted, even lingering in some for a while. Sometimes they stayed in the most unanticipated settings. And so Sheila and Ann wrote about these places to help us interpret the world around us. The paintings and prose in this exhibit are the spiritual icons of the places in our lives where we have crossed the threshold into the sacred.

The show also involved the students in my upper-division theology seminar. On one of those rare, crisp fall sun-drenched days, I took my students to Sheila's studio. She gave us a very quick lesson in drawing, in the many "apps" of the pencil when put to paper: how to shade, point, draw sharp lines. With paper and pencil in hand, we walked over to her neighbor's land and hiked out to a small covered bridge and cabin. We paused to look, to listen, and to draw a bit. Several weeks later the students recalled this trip to the prairie, and all agreed that drawing provided another way to think about the geography of their faith—a way different from reading yet another book I had assigned. At the end of the semester, they wrote marvelously of what they loved about the land, about their faith, about learning to see.

A couple months after the art show opened, Sheila and I were asked by a colleague who teaches in our honors program to come and talk with the students about our art show. The course in which we spoke is titled 'Reading Augustana.' When we asked what the course was about, several students said that they were learning to read and interpret places just as they learned to read and interpret texts. One of their assignments for the course was to pick a spot on campus that becomes theirs. The student is to be in that place on a regular basis to observe, listen, and reflect. The instructor wondered whether by talking about our exhibit, we could help the students connect to this place. She asked us, based on our experiences of getting to know a place, what her students might do to learn more deeply about the place they had chosen to interpret for the course. I suggested that they find another way to learn about the place—a different way from the way they are used to learning. I mentioned to them that I was originally trained and educated as a musician and now as a theologian. I listened and wrote. I didn't really see things. Sheila described to the students what happened when we would hang out at our favorite place down at Dock 44 on the Missouri River, near Platte, South Dakota. We would set out for the day with dogs and her plein air paint, and would sit on the boat. She told them about all the words that I used to describe the scene in front of us and how she painted *blue*. For Sheila, it's about the light. For both of us, it's about paying attention. I felt like the blind man in the passage from the Gospel of Mark. It is taking me stages and several attempts, to learn to see again. Learning to see with the help of Sheila's paintings, I experienced a conversion or transformation of sorts. This conversion might simply be thought of in one word: awareness.

I've been in places I didn't know about, that now I want to see again and again: Blood Run (on the Iowa side); the fifth hole of the Canton Golf Course where the memorial for the Hiawatha Asylum for Insane Indians stands; Gitchie Manitou, the petrified forest in Lemmon, South Dakota;[6] the bird feeders in my backyard; the stretch of trail at Beaver Creek where it turns down onto the bridge over the waters that run in the early spring or that flood during summer rains; the Falls on the Big Sioux; the docks down at Snake Creek on the Missouri River; the East Fork Trail of the Main Boulder in southern Montana; the streets of Hyde Park in Chicago. Now that spring is once again returning in slow and incremental ways, I hope to revisit the small places that made my sabbatical so enchanting and settled, but this time I will catch sight of a hawk on a bur-oak tree branch instead of simply watching another bird on another tree.

Over the last year or two I have become more aware of how little I know, how few things I know the names of, and how little I remember. About the same time that I started going to Sheila's studio, I bought a new camera. I didn't want to fuss with a fancy SLR model but simply wanted something better than the one I often carried in my purse or back pocket. When I mentioned that I had a new camera to a friend of mine, she in turn recommended a book that she thought I might need to read. She must have known that my usual zeal would send me snapping pictures everywhere, taking them as trophies of the visual. I found the title of the recommended book intriguing and ordered it: *The Little Book of Contemplative Photography: Seeing with Wonder, Respect, and Humility*, by Howard Zehr. Knowing how uncontemplative I really am and how obsessed I can become with something, I set the book on the shelf and began going on drives in the country taking all kinds of pictures. By very amateurish standards, some were even good. I even got an honorable

---

6. Surely one of the strangest places on earth.

mention in our local outdoor catalogue's pet-photo competition for my picture of Jack. I called the photograph *Poodle on the Prairie*. Jack's head popped out of the far left, from a high green grassy prairie knob that we had hiked up on a hot summer day. However, as time wore on, I began to get a bit tired of taking my camera along on our evening drives, and weekend hikes. I couldn't stop anywhere without feeling like I had to take pictures. I was on sabbatical, and already I had turned a new pastime into a task—something to accomplish. Then I remembered the book my friend had told me to read.

I skimmed the book and found that the photography is more "about *process* more than *product*."[7] I should know that: I studied process theology. The author contrasts the metaphor of "taking" pictures or "shooting" pictures with "receiving" pictures. I took note of that, once again feeling guilty that I had been "shooting" and "taking" instead of "receiving." But then what really caught my attention was this quote in the chapter titled "An Attitude of Wonder." The author writes: "Years ago my undergraduate philosophy professor, Delbert Wiens, began the semester with an observation that I never forgot and that has deeply influenced me. Instead of Descartes' stance of doubt, he urged us to approach life and the world with an attitude of wonder. An attitude of wonder begins with appreciation rather than suspicion, acknowledging the limits of what we know."[8] No wonder (or pun intended) that once again I couldn't see the world around me. Jesus heals, and the blind *receive* a gift of sight. Zehr suggests what I needed to learn: "An attitude of wonder suggests a stance of openness, a beginner's mind, an embrace of surprises, and ability to live with a degree of uncertainty and unknowing. An attitude of wonder requires that we look anew at the familiar, that we stop taking the world around us for granted. An attitude of wonder acknowledges how little we really know. An attitude of wonder is essential if we are truly to experience the creation and the creator."[9] When I take pictures or shoot pictures, I am able only to see the subject in the picture as an object, something to be taken in through my viewfinder. When I let the object in my lensfinder become the subject of the picture, I find that my frame of reference changes. The view finds me instead. I might call this a vision of grace. I have no idea what it is like to be blind, to not be able to see. However, in

---

7. Zehr, *The Little Book of Contemplative Photography*, 6.
8. Ibid., 33.
9. Ibid.

An Incarnational Methodology

my limited experience, I do know that I do not always receive the world with open eyes or heart. Even those of us who have eyes to see and ears to hear still need to receive from God the gift of grace.

Intense vision is often associated with the mystics. In a blog entry I received from a friend, who periodically knows I need to listen to these kinds of words, I read the following: "The final word for mysticism, after the optimistic explosion that we usually call hope and the ensuing sense of safety, is an experience of deep *rest*. It's the verb I'm told that is most used by the mystics: 'resting in God.' All this striving and this need to perform, climb, and achieve becomes, on some very real level, unnecessary. It's already here, now. I can stop all this overproduction and over-proving of myself. That's Western and American culture. It's not the Gospel at all."[10] Performing, climbing, achieving. For me, those are words of exhaustion; they empty me of life. Resting, recognizing, and receiving. These are gospel words. These will become the rhythms of my life: resting and receiving. They are gifts of sight, of faith.

Julian of Norwich received revelations, visions of God. She wrote them down as *Showings of Love*. With her famous line that "all shall be well, and all manner of things shall be well," Norwich viewed God as gracious and compassionate, and faith received this God with joy and love, not out of fear or duty. In a modern parallel story by Mark Salzman titled *Lying Awake*, Sister John of the Cross is a Carmelite nun who has special visions accompanied by intense and searing headaches. She learns that her visions are the result of temporal lobe epilepsy from a small meningioma. She struggles with the scientific and religious explanations of her visions. Finally she succumbs to surgery and has the small tumor removed, and she loses the intense religious experience. She lives a duller life, one without the intensity of the visions. Instead she gains a different kind of sight, one that resembles the mundane, the everyday, and has to trust in a different kind of grace. The eyes of faith let us pause to take in the extraordinary grace of the ordinary world. "What is saving my life now is the conviction that there is no spiritual treasure to be found apart from the bodily experiences of human life on earth . . . what is saving my life now is becoming more fully human, trusting that there is no way to God apart from real life in the real world."[11]

---

10. Adapted from Rohr, *Following the Mystics through the Narrow Gate*, April 19, 2012.

11. Taylor, *An Altar in the World*, xv.

The Geography of God's Incarnation

I am learning that to think and learn in a theological way doesn't always mean that I must read and write about the texts and traditions of my Christian faith. I can also approach the world with an open posture, letting my senses be my guide, receiving with grace what God gives me in that moment. My experience bears this out: how different the Christian faith looked, sounded, smelled, and felt when I worshiped in a Russian Orthodox congregation in St. Petersburg several years ago. I felt as if my whole being were afire with harmonies, light, and smell. Brilliant mosaic tiles in blue, gold, red and green filled the dome of the sanctuary. The incarnation became incandescent in women's voices, in candles lit. In another church, this time at St. John's Abbey, a Benedictine monastery in Collegeville, Minnesota, I learn about the sacramental presence of God as I chant the Psalms with monks, whose slower and quieter pace calm my spirit. The sanctuary, designed by Marcel Brauer, was radical for its pre–Vatican II time. The massive altar grounds the space, and brightly colored panes of glass transform the back into a beehive of images, representing the Benedictine value of work. Down the road a few miles is the women's monastery where I have attended Sunday Eucharist. Without fail, when I enter the gathering space, which is filled with light and greenery, I am welcomed into the sanctuary. The space is constructed with native granite and imported Bavarian glass. I let the clear voices of the nuns wash over me as they sing the Alleluia in this place. Every fiber of my being is on fire with their presence. The word *incarnation* comes to life through the prayers, psalms, and presence of these gracious women.

Several years ago I traveled to see where some illuminated manuscripts had been made—incandescent texts of incarnation. In the mid-1990s, I went with a group of students and another faculty member to the British Museum to see the Lindisfarne Gospels, illuminated manuscripts created sometime in the early 700s CE at the monastery of Lindisfarne. Likely they were made in honor of St. Cuthbert, a bishop of Lindisfarne sent to the "holy island" to advise the community and to continue missionary work on the nearby mainland. Cuthbert eventually led an aescetic life and moved to one of the smaller islands near Lindisfarne. He was known for blessing visitors and protecting the local wildlife, particularly the birds. During his life, tensions arose between Roman and Celtic ways of Christianity. St. Wilfrid, a supporter of Roman Christianity, eventually helped to defeat Celtic Christianity at the Synod of Whitby. Today communities at both Iona and Lindisfarne continue their Celtic Christian heritage through the offerings of worship and retreats.

An Incarnational Methodology

I was very impressed while looking at the illuminated manuscripts, under glass, in the British Museum, but I became inspired by them when I actually went to the holy island of Lindisfarne. The trip there and back is tricky because of tidewaters that block the causeway between the mainland and the island. As we drove out to Lindisfarne after the tide had receded on the causeway, I could see what looked like large baskets perched on tall sticks. Our coach driver explained that they were for pilgrims along the way who got caught in the tides. They would climb up the posts, perch in the baskets, and safely wait out the tidewaters until they could return to the mainland. When we arrived at Lindisfarne, we ambled along the rugged coastal edge, worn by the cold waters of the North Sea. I thought about how barren and stark the life must have been for those faith monastic artists who etched filigree of gold and other brilliant colors into images and words of the Christian texts. These gospels are windows into the divine, exploding with color, detail, and beauty.

In my own tradition, Martin Luther emphasized again and again that Jesus Christ is the center of the Christian faith, and nothing else. And even *sola scriptura* was interpreted by Luther through his use of a little German phrase, *was Christum treibt*: "that which preaches Christ." For Luther, nothing more directly conveyed the immediate experience of faith than his understanding of what it meant to be church: hearing the Word preached, and receiving sacraments. Second to the preached Word was music—both auditory events, both active experiences. Luther loved the arts and worked closely with artists like Albrecht Durer. When other Reformers around him wanted to enter the Roman Catholic sanctuaries, and smash their so-called idols to bits, Luther objected. Luther was *not* opposed to the use of images; he was opposed to Christians offering worship or adoration to the images instead of to God. Luther even edited the first commandment of the Decalogue, simply leaving out the part about "graven images." As I am learning on this Christian journey, faith is active, alive, and sensuous—incarnational to the fullest extent. Seeing is a portal into the experience of the divine. Long before people wrote texts, they used images.

Nothing brought this to my awareness more than my encounter with some petroglyphs in a remote canyon near Edgemont, South Dakota. On a drive through Red Canyon Road we started our search for the elusive Petroglyphs, one of the destinations on our tour of the sixty-six county destinations in the *South Dakota Magazine*. Several times we got out of the vehicle and walked along the edges of the reddish rocks, kicking up dust on a fall day. Finally, my husband called out, and he had located some of the carvings etched softly into the rock walls. The magazine article had said they were possibly two thousand years old—writings on a wall from around the same time that the writings of the Christian Scripture were etched onto parchment. I have no idea what the images meant or who carved them into the wall. What I did sense was that for some people, in a distant past in this rough-walled canyon, images were left as texts, to be viewed and interpreted by others. I was suddenly seized by a sense of awe; I was up, close, and personal with the writing on the wall. I felt some distant connection to this incarnation of a people's thoughts carved into the rocks of their surroundings. That deep sense of awe changed into amusement when a few minutes later we saw another carving: this time it was a man's name and a date, from the late 1800s. This wild canyon road had once been a stagecoach road, carrying gamblers to and from Deadwood, South Dakota. The images spoke to me of ancestors, together in this land of rock, hard edges, red dust, and adventure. My job that hot fall day was to interpret what they meant to me. I became a student of hermeneutics, reading not words in a book, but images made from rock and red dust: a hermeneutics of the visible.[12]

A colleague of mine, a poet and lover of the English language, referred me to the theologian who coined this term *the hermeneutics of the visible*. Diana Eck, who is also a native of my hometown of Bozeman, Montana, wrote about the hermeneutics of the visible in her book titled *Darsan: Seeing the Divine Image in India*. Eck claims that her excursion into Hinduism is a visual one: *darsan* is the way into the divine. "When Hindus go to the temple, their eyes meet the powerful, eternal gaze of the eyes of God. It is called *darsan*, 'seeing' the divine image, and it is the single most common and significant element of Hindu worship."[13] Based on her understanding and experiences of Hinduism, Eck develops a "hermeneutic of the visible."[14] She explains that Hindus in India have religious experiences that come through seeing the divine, and seeing is also a way of knowing and learning. We know the world from the way we see the world. Our world "views" are thoughtful constructions of the visible. Where we stand literally determines what we see. In some strange way, I also understand that I have also encountered the divine through seeing.

---

12. Eck, *Darsan*, 1.
13. Ibid
14. Ibid, 14.

An Incarnational Methodology

My hermeneutic of the visible has not come through my experience of Hinduism but through the experiences I have had in the natural world, from the creation of God. In another of her books, *Encountering God: From Bozeman to Banaras*, Eck writes about how life in the mountains of the west shaped her understanding of Christianity. (Her father was the Methodist pastor in a church down the street from where I worshiped.) Like me, she spent her summers at camp in the mountains, which shaped how she experienced her Christian faith. The mountains were as important to both of us as were the texts we read and the hymns we sang on Sunday mornings. Whether the images come through paintings, icons, photographs, or films, the way we see the world creates the way we interpret the world. Drawing on the philosophy of Rudolf Arnheim, Eck claims that the images we see with our eyes shape the thoughts we have about our world, and not the other way around. We bring our body-selves and our past with us, so to speak, when we see the world. We don't look *at*. We see *with*. Eck writes: "Seeing, after all, is an imaginative, constructive activity, an act of making. It is not simply the reception of images on the retina."[15]

What is even more fascinating to me is Eck's observations, via other writers, that perception is a form of thinking per se. We use words such as *insight* or *vision*, or phrases such as *point of view* to describe what we are thinking. Thought and sight are intimately related. They are not as distinct and disjunctive as we modern Cartesian Westerners might want to claim. "The making of all those images is the fundamental 'imaginative' human activity. One might add that it is the fundamental activity of the religious imagination as well."[16] This brings to mind the language of prehensions, from Alfred North Whitehead; *prehension* is a word that he used to talk about grasping or reaching out when we take in the world around us. And we bring our past (*causal efficacy* for the Whiteheadians) with us. We look at images differently, depending on our past, our cultural expectations, and our experiences of ourselves as bodies. Eck explains that when we see the images of another culture, we must realize that we often see them without models to help us recognize and understand them within their context. Our own visual models do not often transfer to other models. We have to learn how to see. We have to know context and the point of view. "Without such self-conscious questioning, we cannot begin to 'think' with what we see and we simply dismiss it as

15. Ibid.
16. Ibid.

strange. Or worse, we are bound to misinterpret what we see by placing it solely within the context of what we already know from our own world of experience."[17] That is why we need to see through another's eyes.

If we fail to look with and through someone else's eyes and images, we can become xenophobic, seeing their images as idols. Eck, I believe, rightly explains that there is a Western antagonism to worshiping the divine through images. The Reformers' fear of worshiping God through images finds its root deeply embedded in the Christian tradition. "The Hebraic resistance to imaging the divine has combined with a certain distrust of the sense in the world of the Greek tradition as well."[18] Eck claims that the religions of the West have "trusted the Word more than the Image as a mediator of the divine truth."[19] How true that has been for me! I have been taught to hear the word, not to see the Word. And yet Western Christianity is not completely without images. Eck reminds me about the beautiful illuminated manuscripts I have traveled to see: The Book of Kells, the Lindisfarne Gospels, and the contemporary St. John's Bible. While the Orthodox tradition of iconography and the Catholic traditions of the visual arts is present in the Christian tradition, as a Protestant I have been warned to not worship these images lest they become idols of my faith. After all, Christendom supposedly split over the use of icons. The presence of God is never to be simply reduced to one place or person or sense. God is always more. Diane Eck warns us, however, in the history of the Christian West, when we use the word *idols* to describe what others worship, the language is always about them. Her warning is important.

Learning to see with the eyes of Sheila's art and through her landscapes of the plains has made me realize how impoverished my own gallery of the world has been. In one of my favorite books, *Lydia Cassatt Reading the Morning Paper*, about Lydia and her sister, the famous artist Mary Cassatt, I came across this quote: "Such sensations make me think of my girlhood. I look closely at each memory, in my own gallery, as if to discover some clue, some fresh element in the story: a hand on an arm, a glove left on an arm, a glance, a glove left on a seat, maybe."[20] Harriett Chessman crafts a touching story about how Lydia learns to live within the confines of terminal illness while she also watches the paintings of her

17. Ibid., 16.
18. Ibid., 18.
19. Ibid., 20.
20. Chessman, *Lydia Cassatt Reading the Morning Paper*, 23.

famous artist sister unfold each day. Each chapter centers on a painting, and as the story unfolds, readers begin to recall their own life's pictures, told through the stories of their gallery. As I observed Sheila's gallery of paintings unfold each day, the images of the landscape around me and their accompanying narratives became richer and more nuanced.

When I crossed the threshold from my daily life into the world of Sheila's artwork, I experienced a transformation, a conversion of seeing life with new eyes. Esther De Waal, a favorite English spiritual writer of mine, explains what happens when we cross thresholds, when we leave one place and move across the door and into another place: "It means taking the risk that old certainties might be replaced by a new way of seeing the world. Another word is conversion, not in the relatively easy sense of changing to religion, or from one denomination to another, but in the much more demanding sense of 'turning around,' and 'discovering that there's a whole world out there you hadn't really been aware of.'"[21] Working with Sheila on our joint exhibit became this kind of conversion for me. I didn't realize it until it happened; it didn't happen all at once. My eyes weren't suddenly opened. I'm still a visual neophyte. But I'm aware, taking notice of how much more I know about my Christian faith now that I have learned to notice the world around me.

After watching Sheila Agee's paintbrush bring the prairie landscape to life and light, I have become aware of how much art really brings the Word of God to life and to light. Not only has my eyesight improved, but also other senses are heightened, as if my eye has become the portal through which the other senses are aware. My road trips have become pilgrimages of the visual. I am a pilgrim of the Image, mirrored in the landscapes of creation as the incarnation of God. During a recent drive northward toward Pierre, the state capital of South Dakota, my husband and I watched the sun slowly sink behind the bluffs along the Missouri River. The next morning we left the hotel, urged our sleepy dogs into the vehicle, and headed north to our new favorite sanctuary in South Dakota: the Little Bend Recreation Area. Although we didn't arrive right at sunrise, the early morning light was still firing the low hills and bluffs that stretched for miles on three sides of us. The Missouri River was quiet, spreading out for miles into a mirror of stillness. Pale pinks and oranges highlighted the bluffs reflected in the water. This scene reminded me of the paintings of the northern plains and the Missouri River of Montana

---

21. De Waal, *To Pause at the Threshold*, 8.

by Charlie Russell that I had seen as a child. I remember that the colors were often muted, pale and quiet. Now, on this quiet, almost desolate landscape in central South Dakota, I think I understood his work, literally in a new light. Light and illumination are part of the landscapes of my faith.

I have changed the way I see because I have been given new eyes, through the grace of God and with the help of others. What I was once blind to will now appear as forms, as "trees walking," the Gospel of Mark says. With practice I can sharpen my vision, while I continue on this pilgrimage of sight. The forms in life that appear like "trees walking," that seem to be only contrasts of diffused light and shadow, will slowly come into focus, and I will see this creation around me in new ways. In another gospel story about learning to see and walking on the way, we meet the disciples, on the road to Emmaus, and Jesus appears to them. The disciples too had trouble seeing. The text says: "their eyes were kept from recognizing him." After a lengthy exchange of questions and answers, the disciples invite Jesus, whom they still don't recognize, to stop and stay with them, and break bread. And then in the breaking, blessing, and eating of the bread, they recognize Jesus, and immediately he vanishes from their sight. In order to see, we are required to meet along the road, and share our bread with one another. When we the take time to notice who our companions are, then and only then will we see where we are and who is with us. In the flesh and blood, in the breaking of the body and the sharing of the cup, we know whose we are and where we are—God finds God's home in us.

4

Grounding Incarnation in Creation
We Begin in the Cathedral of God's Creation and Move through the Local Sites

EXCURSUS

A Traveler's Manifesto for Navigating the Creation

*I*BELIEVE THAT WHAT THE *world needs is a fresh spiritual road map that can shape and inform a new and powerful way of helping us to navigate and interpret our place within the universe, from both cosmic and familial perspectives. And this spiritual vision must be told as a story, so we can find ourselves within it. The Epic of Evolution is a place to start. And as a Christian, I believe that God is present in the creatures of the entire cosmos. Genesis 1, John 1, and Colossians 1 reveal, albeit in somewhat different ways, the same epic narrative of our evolution.*

We are created critters—companion species of God's own making. John 3:16 should be retranslated: For God so loved the cosmos. God's love is so much bigger, wider, and deeper than I can ever imagine. Martin Luther wrote that God is present both in the veins of a leaf and in the elements of the Eucharist. Our worldly table is set with bread and wine. Doxologies seem appropriate for such a credo: Thanks be to God for this most amazing world.

The Geography of God's Incarnation

I was born in 1957, the same year that Sputnik was launched by the Russians, what we now consider the beginning of the space age. From the middle of the twentieth century through the late 1990s, Russians and Americans competed to occupy this new frontier. Americans walked in space and sent men to the moon. Billions of dollars were spent on the exploration of outer space. Simultaneously, biotechnological and scientific advances propelled us into the intricate tissues, organs, bones, and other structures of the human being. As the 1990s drew to a close, and so did the funding for the space age, we have ventured into the new territory of the World Wide Web. The space age has been replaced by the information age. All these technological and scientific travels, to the farthest reaches of outer space and to the inner workings of the human brain, make me question my place in the universe. On the one hand, I feel like the center of the universe, knowing that I'm part of a unique species who can accomplish so much. On the other hand, I appear to be nothing more than a speck of cosmic dust, painfully aware of how vast the universe is, how little we really know about it, and how small a part of it I really am. We are not so very different from the explorers who went before us. Our odysseys are recorded now on YouTube videos rather than in epic tales by the Greeks. But the universal human quest for meaning tells us that we always yearn for something more. We want to lean into the future of our becoming, while trying to hold onto the moorings of our past and present. As we set out on our epic journeys of discovery, we rely on the familiar maps and landmarks that have oriented our lives. Who are we? Where are we? How then shall we live? Sometimes the world is changing so fast that we barely articulate the questions, let alone try to respond adequately to them.

These are questions not only about the meaning of the being and becoming of human identity, but also about the nature and action of God's grace in the world. The words from John 3:16, "For God so loved the cosmos," take on new meaning in light of our scientific and technological awareness. The history of Christian theology addresses these questions from at least three loci: the doctrine of creation, the interpretation of the *imago Dei*, and the doctrine of the incarnation. It is no surprise to Christians that the center of the incarnation is the person of Jesus Christ. But it might be a stretch for some Christians to imagine that the promise that God has become flesh is not only in a person but also in a place, in the creation. For Christian theology, the *imago Dei* is the doctrine that explains the relationship of humans to God, and this doctrine has been

Grounding Incarnation in Creation

used almost exclusively to reveal that humans alone are created in the image of God. As we shall see, this narrow interpretation fails to explain not only our relationship to God but also our relationship to ourselves and the rest of creation. Christian theologians need to expand the notion of what incarnation means, and what it means to be created in the image of God so that the scope of God's creative and redemptive action and work indeed reaches the breadth of all things—from the outer reaches of space to the inner reaches of our hearts.[1] Otherwise, our understanding of God's work is constricted by our fears of extending it beyond our reach. So, I ask again: Who are we? Where are we? And how then shall we live? This perspective hopefully means more than what the popular bumper sticker reveals: think globally, act locally. We must live and travel in both the cosmic and local realms at the same time. If we ignore one or the other, we can be become displaced. To be the creature of God that God calls us to be requires a kind of dual citizenship—within the details of our daily life, attending to the needs of our neighbors, while always knowing we are part of a much greater cosmos whose future is still unfolding.

The Local with Cosmic Implications

To figure out who I am, I decided to go to Iowa (isn't that what most people do?), via the outskirts of Sioux Falls. On a warm spring day, I downloaded some directions and map from my trusted website, MapQuest, to help orient myself as I took my technojourney from the urban landscapes of Sioux Falls to the farms and fields of Iowa. The first destination, the corporate headquarters of Sanford Research, is located on the very edge of Sioux Falls near the interstate. I drove in on the road marked by a sign in the Sanford blue, which simply said, "Road to the Cure." The road sign is placed near the sign demarcating the start of the center's property. In addition to the name of the corporation, Sanford Research, this sign bears the slogan "Dedicated to the Work of Health and Healing." Once a month I drive from my home to this sprawling health-care landscape, which is surrounded by white rail fences, duck ponds, and neatly trimmed lawns. When I enter the building, I often feel like an interloper in this world of scientific research. But that is my purpose, to come as the

---

1. Gilkey, "Nature as the Image of God," 127–41. I am indebted to Langdon Gilkey for his constructive interpretation of nature as the image of God. He wrote: "My theme is the theologically deviant but nonetheless important suggestions that nature represents an *imago dei*, an image and likeness of its divine creator" (127).

outside member on the institutional research board (IRB) for Sanford. On its website, Sanford claims the following: "We are changing the landscape of science and health care. Our growing team of more than 200 researchers is focused on identifying new therapies and treatments for some of the world's leading health concerns. It's our goal to find solutions that will cure illness, eradicate disease and improve the lives of people in our communities and around the world."[2] I have friends who work on breast cancer research while others hope to find a cure for Type I diabetes. Sanford is literally and figuratively changing the landscape of the area through the technologies that scientists use on the roads to finding new cures. I am limited by what I don't know, so I can only imagine, when I enter this building, what happens in the labs. But I do know that the research in medicine and health care is changing the landscape of what it means to be human in ways that most of us still think of as happening only in some kind of Hollywood action movie.

In another Sanford building, closer to my home, the researchers in human reproductive medicine are housed. I have met the scientists who practice reproductive endocrinology, and have listened to them describe the amazing research. Babies are created, made *in vitro* from donor sperm and donor eggs. Embryos can be implanted in gestational surrogates. Now with the recent advances in the sciences of genetics, embryos are genetically screened for potential lethal anomalies. Who are we? And where are we? Sometimes it feels like we're in a land of science fiction and venturing into worlds we barely know or understand. And yet all of these human reproductive technological advances begin somewhere else, most likely in the fields of Iowa or in veterinary laboratories.

I continue my technojourney as I leave the headquarters of Sanford Research to head south and east. As I drive through the rolling fields near the Big Sioux River, I cross the South Dakota border and into Iowa. About forty-five miles away, after taking country roads right and then left, I find another corporate landscape: Trans Ova Genetics. This one, however, is not urban. The complex is surrounded by large metal gates and rails, and I see hundreds of cattle with tags on their ears. They munch on hay, glaring at me as I drive by. Trans Ova's website explains its mission: "To become the global leader in the application of innovative and reproductive technology." Their vision is "to serve our clients by assisting them in increasing the

---

2. Website. Online: http://www.sanfordresearch.org/.

Grounding Incarnation in Creation

genetic impact of their 'success' in their breeding programs."[3] Trans Ova uses some of the same reproductive technologies that the Sanford Health Fertility and Reproductive lab does: embryo transfer and *in vitro* fertilization (IVF). But Trans Ova also clones cattle and "works closely with clients to understand their breeding goals, and ultimately help clients advance and extend superior genetics."[4] What happens in the barns and labs of Trans Ova is only a field or two away from the human labs of Sanford Research. If indeed we are related to all creation, then I understand what it means to be created in wholly and maybe holy new ways. Reproductive technologies move from nonhuman to human in just a few small steps. In some weird way, I both feel and know that I'm related to these cattle. In fields not far from Trans Ova are the transgenic cattle created at Hematech.[5] Inside a circle of about seventy-five miles, I am learning that what it means to be a creature of God is much more complicated than I ever imagined.

While I have discovered that the world around me is much bigger, deeper, and wider than I could have guessed, I have also learned that it is much smaller, more intimately related, and complicated than I can comprehend. I have traveled to places which have redefined for me what it means to be a creature, to be created, and to be related to the rest of the world! I claim that what we have understood by the *imago Dei*, to be created in the image of God, is much too small and constricted. If being created in the image of God has something to do with our relationships with other creatures, then this is the place from which we will start our exploration of the *imago Dei*. Langdon Gilkey clarifies this in a helpful way: "In this context, image is taken to mean a sign, symbol, or sacrament of the divine, disclosing through itself the divine glory."[6] Places like the Sanford Research Center and Trans Ova are strange worlds indeed; new maps are required for navigating these new worlds, these technoscapes. So, if I am going to venture into strange new worlds, I want to do so as those who have gone before me have done, with the tools and companionship of fellow travelers. Christians before me have used two books as sources to navigate the cosmic in their quests for meaning: the book of nature and the book of Scripture. These sources have shaped the way we interpret the theological doctrines of incarnation and *imago Dei*. Now, we must revisit

---

3. Website. Online: http://www.transova.com/company.html/.
4. Ibid.
5. Sanford Research. "Sanford Applied Biosciences."
6. Gilkey, "Nature as the Image of God," 127.

and reinterpret the old sources of the Christian faith in light of this wild world that we have just explored (albeit via the farms of Iowa).

Becoming Reacquainted with and Reinterpreting Two Familiar Landmarks of the Christian Faith

The Book of Nature, and the Book of Scripture

We are creatures, made by God, called to give thanks and worship our Creator, while at the same time loving and honoring the creation that God made for us. The world is God's temple. We stand on holy ground, and most of us don't even know it! We are humans, created by God, for relationship with all that is, in this very real world. Who are we? And where are we? Our answers depend on our perspective, on what we see from where we stand. From the galactic solar systems to the veins of our bodies, I propose that we take an excursion through this universe. Throughout the ages, poets, priests, artists, and scientists have listened to, observed, and meditated on the wonders of creation. They have practiced the art of *lectio divina,* a contemplative form of prayer, by paying careful attention to and interpreting the two great books of the Christian tradition: the book of nature and the book of sacred Scripture. These two sources meld together in the following words from St. Paul's letter to the Romans: "Ever since the creation of the world his eternal power and divine nature, invisible though they are, have been understood and seen through the things he has made. So they are without excuse."[7] Let us take St. Paul's warning seriously and find no excuse! We must read and pay careful attention to the living Word of God in nature and to living Word of God in the texts we call the Holy Scriptures.

Many early patristic scholars connected the Word of God as Christ to the word of God in Scripture. The Word of God in Christ is the same Word who creates the world. (John 1, Colossians 1) St. Irenaeus "holds that everything is created in the Son, and thus secures a theological way to hold nature and grace together. The Word in which all is created is the same Verbum which became flesh in Christ. This makes it possible to go from the revelation of God in the Son to a corollary and further revelation of the Father in nature."[8] We can practice the art of *lectio divina* with

---

7. Rom 1:21 (NRSV).

8. Sittler, *Essays on Nature and Grace,* 57–58.

the Christian Scriptures, but also with the other great book: the book of nature. Nature and grace come together in the reading of the Word of God in Christ.

When I have traveled to St. John's Monastery in Collegeville, Minnesota, I have learned how Benedictine monks practice the ancient arts of calligraphy and illumination to make the Word of God come alive. The words literally jump off the page with vivacity and perspicuity. Standing in the Hill Museum and Manuscript Library at St. John's University, I have read selected pages of the new St. John's Bible. Although, I must say, that the reading is more akin to looking. Completed on September 15, 2011, "The Saint John's Bible is a work of art and a work of theology . . . The result is a living document and a monumental achievement."[9] The brilliantly colored artwork illuminates the words of Scripture, words that I have often ignored when they are simply printed on the page. The Word is created by those who practice the art of *lectio divina*. Instead of listening to the Word through the prayers of monks in worship, I am watching the Word becoming flesh through the strokes of artists.

In what I would consider another form of *lectio divina*, I have watched Sheila Agee, a prairie artist, paint the book of nature with broad strokes, forming them into patterns, focusing them into a vast landscape. Each day she retouches the painting, adding depth and shape. Layers upon layers reveal the Word of God. This prairie artist has helped me to read anew the great book of nature, God's creation. Each day and week my interpretation changes, along with the rhythms and seasons of the land. This is a different kind of *lectio divina*, a reading of the creation done with my eyes opened by the grace of God. The creation echoes Augustine's famous words: "Look above you! Look below you! Note it. Read it." As I gaze at the painting, I notice the stalks of corn, planted row by row. This will be my next hermeneutical challenge, a chapter of creation just waiting to be read!

To open the book of nature is to venture into a landscape of vast dimensions and microscopic elements. We use giant telescopes to explore the galaxies that spiral into an ever-expanding universe and powerful microscopes to examine the DNA in our cells, the map of our human genome. And located somewhere between the infinite reaches of the universe and the minute strands of DNA are human beings. I can only respond with wonder, amazement, and mystery. I am both a child of God

9. "The Process."

created to be on this planet called Earth, and a child of the universe that is still on its voyage to becoming something new. Scientists remind us that the journey of the universe from its inception in the big bang until now has taken approximately fourteen to fifteen billion years and the process is still unfolding. I'm both on my own journey through my lifetime, trying to make sense of it all, and also part of a much larger voyage, God's voyage, that is moving in, with, and under me.[10] The large and small of it, somewhere in between (*in medias res*) is that we are travelers on the way, looking upward and heavenward, inward and internally.

Another way to read or interpret the book of nature is to do so up, close, and personal: on foot, with backpack, stepping into the wilderness. During the summers when I led the flatlanders from Minnesota and the Dakotas into the mountains of Montana and Colorado, my tools for finding the way were a compass, topographical maps, cairns, and most of all, paying close attention to where I was so that if I got lost, I could recall the details of my surroundings. Many of the trails we followed had been carved into the hillside decades before, and were marked by the blazes on the trails. But weather and time had taken their toll, and the marks on those trails faded into the dense stands of lodgepole pines and the carefully placed cairns had collapsed. Eventually I would lose my way and have to take a detour or create a trail of my own.

I've been afraid to take the detour, to let the digressions become the way. Our market-driven culture demands that we can't afford to spend precious time leisurely going here and there. Yet, here and there is precisely where the trails in our life might take us. We have lost the ability to go astray, to veer off course. As Jim Bridger is reported to have said, "I wasn't lost; I just didn't know where I was for a few weeks."[11] We all need to learn how to wander here and there, to go along just for the ride, or the hike, in this case. It's not that we are lost; it's just that we don't know where we are at the moment. And where are we? The answer to that question is the quest itself, the detour, the path where we can go astray. If we can let go of always being on the main highway, we might discover that the detours, side roads, and backcountry might be the best way to get to know the universe both inside and outside of us.

For many Christians the main highway has been the Jesus way, and the main tool to navigate this way is the Bible: the Word of God.

---

10. I am grateful to Philip Hefner for this image. Hefner, *The Human Factor*, 55–56.
11. Batson, *Michael Batson: Travel Writer*.

Grounding Incarnation in Creation

However, I want to claim that the Christian tradition offers multiple ways to navigate our faith with God and the world. We might begin with Jesus the Christ, but we can also begin in creation, in the world created by the Word of God incarnate. However, since I believe that too many Christians focus so much on the person of Jesus that they don't notice the world around them, I believe that the doctrine of creation might be the theological detour we need to take in order to fully understand what it means to be on the road with Jesus. Our navigation tools will include not only the Christian Scriptures but also the book of nature interpreted through the eyes, ears, and words of scientists, poets, musicians, and naturalists. Places become sacred texts that we will read and interpret just like we do the texts from Scripture. The creation way might just become the way to understand the Way. Jesus said, "I am the way, the truth, and the life." The way to this truth is through the Jesus Way, who is also the firstborn of all creation, the one in whom all things were created and hold together. This Word is our compass for orienting our way through creation.

Creation is the starting place from which I navigate and interpret the message that God so loves this cosmos, that God gave God's only son. The theologian that has blazed the theological trail for me to understand and interpret what it means to be a creature in God's creation is Joseph Sittler, a Lutheran. Joseph Sittler was, and still is, ahead of his time. In the 1950s and 1960s, he listened to the cultural sirens around him and interpreted their warning calls. Scientists, poets, artists, and writers were all saying the same thing: the planet was in peril. In the wake of World War II, schoolchildren practiced diving under their desks, in case of nuclear attacks. I remember the home my parents bought in the 1960s had a bomb shelter that the previous owners had created. The dank, musty smell there reminded me, even as a child, what death might smell like, a warning that I lived in a world in which I felt very vulnerable. Pete Seeger published his political song, "Where Have All the Flowers Gone?," and Bob Dylan sang his war-protest song, "Blowin' in the Wind." Rachel Carson published her famous book, *The Silent Spring*, in 1962, warning us that chemical pesticides were causing environmental devastation.

During these same turbulent times, in his prophetic address to the World Council of Churches, Sittler warned that the church was not paying attention to these cultural portents that the world was in trouble! Like Dietrich Bonhoeffer, who warned the churches in Nazi Germany, Sittler feared that churches focused only on their own piety and institutional trappings and rituals. Churches were reducing the good news about the wide scope of God's love and grace for the world to the small place of personal salvation and heavenly hereafters. Sittler claimed that the message of the Christian gospel preached and taught in congregations was too small. The cosmic dimensions of God's creative purposes had been lost! According to Sittler, the place in which God's grace was at work was much larger, grander, and wider than we could ever imagine! In other words, when Christians translate John 3:16, they should remember that God so loved the *cosmos,* not just the world of their own personal lives. This slight difference in wording from the usual "For God so loved the world," reminds Christians that God, the Word incarnate, is the God of the whole cosmos. *In the beginning*—the opening words from Genesis reflect the same words that launch St. John's Gospel: "In the Beginning was the Word." The classical Greek and Hebrew poets seemed to have greater imaginations than we often do. While they open worlds with their words, we have used words to close off and constrict our worlds.

The biblical heart of this cosmic Christology is in Colossians 1:15–20 (CEB):

> 15 The Son is the image of the invisible God, the one who is first over all creation, 16 Because all things were created by him: both in the heavens and on the earth, the things that are visible and the things that are invisible. Whether they are thrones or powers, or rulers or authorities, all things were created through him and for him. 17 He existed before all things, and all things are held together in him. 18 He is the head of the body, the church, who is the beginning, the one who is firstborn from among the dead so that he might occupy the first place in everything. 19 Because all the fullness of God was pleased to live in him, 20 and he reconciled all things to himself through him—whether things on earth or in the heavens. He brought peace through the blood of his cross.

Christ is the one in whom God was pleased to live! So, if God is in Christ, and in all things, God is also pleased to live in us! I heard it once said that Martin Luther explained grace this way: when we look into the mirror, we know that we can be pleased with our image, because we are looking into the image of God's gracious love for us. How different we might be if we reflected on this icon of mutual pleasure between God and us.

To explain the cosmic vision of Colossians, Sittler used the image of an orbit. Our redemption is only meaningful when it swings within the

Grounding Incarnation in Creation

bigger orbit of God's creation.[12] Because I think what Sittler was saying is so important, I quote him at some length:

> We must not fail to see the nature and size of the issue that Paul confronts (in Col. 1:15–20) and encloses in this vast Christology. In propositional form it is simply this: *a doctrine of redemption is meaningful only when it swings within the larger orbit of a doctrine of creation. For God's creation of earth cannot be redeemed in any intelligible sense of the word apart from a doctrine of the cosmos which is his home, his definite place, the theater of his selfhood under God, in corporation with his neighbor, and in caring-relationship with nature, his sister* . . . *Unless the reference and the power of the redemptive act includes the whole of human experience and the environment, straight out to its farthest horizon, then the redemption is incomplete. There is and will always remain something of evil to be overcome. And more. Men and women in their existence will be tempted to reduce human redemption to what purgation, transformation, forgiveness, and blessedness is available by an 'angelic' escape from the cosmos of natural and historical fact.*[13]

These words of Sittler shatter our narrow worldviews. In much the same way, scientists have shattered the self-centeredness of our worldview and our seemingly grand place within it. We credit Galileo and Copernicus, who replaced our earth-centered worldview with a heliocentric one. The implications of Darwin's *The Origin of Species* and recent discoveries by Crick, Watson, and Franklin about DNA have charted new territories with maps of the human genome. While we are important actors in the theater of nature, we are not always at center stage. We must interpret this cosmic vision of our place within the larger scope of God's gracious actions in creation. So I take us back to Iowa, to those cattle at Trans Ova. Those transgenic species, created with cattle and human DNA, are our brothers and sisters. And so are the researchers and scientists who have created them. Such complicated relationships are part of this creation of God. Luther says we are called to love and serve our neighbor. Who is our neighbor? I never thought I'd have to travel to Iowa to really understand the implications of that question.

Sittler says we should look to the farthest horizon, and step out with our neighbors, in "caring-relationship with nature," who is our sister and

12. Sittler, "Called to Unity," 40.
13. Ibid.

brother. We are relatives—Brother Sun, Sister Moon, and Mother Earth. St. Francis even says that Brother Sun, of all God's creation, bears the divine likeness! We are one among God's creatures, giving praise to God! But these words are radical to me precisely because I went to Iowa and saw my bovine kin, those in whom the collusion of science, technology, DNA, and God's intentions for the world come together in a crazy, complex family tree of creatureliness.

Years ago I heard a rare thing, a sermon in a Lutheran church on a text from the Apocrypha. Because the sermon and reading of the text from the Wisdom of Solomon 7 and 8 sounded so out of place and startled me, I have decided to keep this text within the canon of my daily life. In this ancient text, God is personified as Woman Wisdom, as divine *Sophia*, whose presence and power extend to all creation. She reflects the image of God's goodness: "For she is a reflection of the working of God, an image of his goodness."[14] In his mediations on nature, John Muir wrote: "To lovers of the wild, these mountains are not a hundred miles away. Their spiritual power and the goodness of the sky make them near, as a circle of friends. You cannot feel yourself out of doors; plain, sky, and mountains ray beauty which you feel. You bathe in these spirit-beams, turning round and round, as if warming at a camp-fire. Presently you lose consciousness of your own separate existence: you blend with the landscape, and become part and parcel of nature."[15] Both the Canticle of St. Francis and the Wisdom of Solomon call us to give praise to the Author of our origins. Who are we? We only have to look around in creation to those to whom we are related to answer that question. In these wonderful texts, we see the image of who we are reflected back to us in the relationships we have with all creation and with God. To be created in the image of God is to be made for relationship with all creation and with God. Sometimes I might wonder about my family tree, whose roots and limbs are expanding with new species: hybrids of machine and human, human and nonhuman, animal and plant. Transgenic and transcultural, my relatives, like me, are companions of God's creating and human co-creating, animal making and machine designing. All of a sudden, my family tree looks much stranger than before, and I'm not sure what a reunion with all creation would be like. What new species have yet to emerge in this crazy

---

14. Wisdom of Solomon 7: 26 (NRSV).

15 Highland, *Meditations of John Muir*, 121.

Grounding Incarnation in Creation

world? What really will it mean to preach and think about a new heaven and a new earth? I have no idea.

Grounded in the Familiar, We Move on to New Paths of Interpreting Our Place in the World

Cosmic Dimensions of Incarnation and Imago Dei.

Now that we are more grounded in the familiar landmarks of the Christian tradition, we can embark on the adventure of expanding our vision of what it means that God is incarnate in the world, and that we are created in the image of God. These two theological loci, reshaped and expanded, will give us new theological definitions to help us to sort out the other important question: how then shall we live? Gregory Peterson, a Lutheran theologian and philosopher, explains that the specific term *image of God* is found in the book of Genesis in three places: 1:26–27; 5:1–13; and 9:1–7. The interpretation of these texts and of this specific doctrine has a long and varied history,[16] and they have been used to differentiate and separate God from humans and from the rest of the creation. However, Peterson makes clear that in our contemporary era, the ecological crisis and the influence of evolutionary sciences have challenged the traditional notion that the *imago Dei* should be confined to human beings. In fact, he along with other theologians like Philip Hefner,[17] and Langdon Gilkey, are saying what I want to claim, which is that all of nature should reflect the image of God's creation. This perspective relocates the *imago Dei* into the landscape of the whole created order. Who we are is related to where we are. Because we come from the *terra firma*, and God is the ground of our being, I define the image of God as the vocation of the created order to be and become freely that which fulfills God's gracious purposes and intentions for the creation. Specifically, for human beings, I use the definition that Philip Hefner uses: humans are created co-creators, and the meaning and purpose of human life comes from their placement within the natural world.[18] We are both free and interdependent with God and all creation. Our vocation is rooted in our location.

---

16. Peterson, "Imago Dei."
17. Hefner, *The Human Factor*, 273.
18. Ibid., 45.

The Geography of God's Incarnation

Where are we? What is our theological GPS location? *Where are you?* is the first question God asks the human beings in the strange land of Eden. After Adam and Eve eat the famous fruit, their eyes are opened, and they know that they are naked, so God provides clothing for them. Later on, in the time of the evening breeze, the Lord God takes a walk, and "the man and his wife hid themselves from the presence of the Lord God among the trees of the garden. But the Lord God called to the man, and said to him, 'Where are you?'"[19] More questions follow. And the tragedy of the garden unfolds. Like our progenitors in Eden, we often find ourselves lost, restless, and ashamed, when we are asked where we are and we don't know how to answer. Nearly all of us have experienced shame, restlessness, fear, anxiety, and confusion when we hide from God; we feel displaced. Our sin can separate us, dis-placing us from our home in God. We no longer (as if we ever did) live in the garden of Eden; we have cast ourselves eastward, out of the garden. The story continues east of Eden with Cain and Abel.

The author of this story knows well that when the tiller of the ground competes with the keeper of the sheep, God will once again ask: "Where is your brother, Abel?" And we have answered: "I do not know; am I my brother's keeper?" The Lord will say to us: "What have you done? Listen; your brother's blood is crying out to me from the ground! And now you are cursed from the ground, which has opened its mouth to receive your brother's blood from your hand. When you till the ground, it will no longer yield to you its strength; *you will be a fugitive and a wanderer on earth.*"[20] We long to be at home in this world, and yet we feel like perpetual wanderers, fugitives on the run. Our mission to be at home in our world seems impossible. We are dis-placed people, sent away from the garden, to wander on the earth.

Part of our own displacement stems from the fact that for too long we have fancied ourselves to be above nature or separate from it. Instead of honoring our call to care for nature, we have dominated, domesticated, and romanticized nature. Nature is the backdrop on the stage in which we are the only stars. But I have tried to establish that such a drama that we act out about ourselves is wrongheaded, even dangerous. We need to get rid of this static, simplistic, hierarchical picture of nature. Instead we must examine more closely the complicated, complex images of

---

19. Genesis 3:9 (NRSV).
20. Genesis 4:9–12 (NRSV).

nature and humans that we find today. For example, when we hike in the wilderness we take our GPS with us. Everywhere we go, we take our gadgets. There is literally no place in the world that remains untouched by humans and human technology.[21] We blend together, nature, technology, humans, and animals. We are not separate but related. We are more like hybrids or mutts, a blending of natural and artificial, human and machine. *Our natural world is technonatural.* We must now have a more dynamic image of what it means that all creation reflects the image of God. We are techno-sapiens rooted and entangled in techno-natures. The *imago Dei* must reflect the cyborgs, hybrids that we really are. The human being has evolved from *Homo sapiens* to techno-sapiens. This, I believe, does not mean that we are less or more human, but that our being and human becoming mean that we are intertwined with, inseparable from, the technologies we use. We need new boundaries and road maps for interpreting the *imago Dei*.[22] We have established the cosmic and global implications of what it means to interpret our place in the world and to be created in the image of God. We can let the cosmic and global perspective shape our local locations.

In, With, and Under

Local Incarnations of Our Technoselves in a Technolandscape

Sioux Falls, South Dakota, the city that I call home, is at the intersection of several different geographies: it lies between two major arterial interstates (where human trafficking happens at the local truck stops), between the urban and the rural, between three different states, between what was once a primarily homogeneous population of Euro-American whites and what is now an ever increasingly diverse population from all over the world, and between biotechnological research firms and two large hospital systems. Parking lots and supersized shopping centers are sites as familiar to the locals as are the fields of corn and soybeans that separate agricultural and urban areas. We live together: all kinds of species in our local environmental niches. In the center of the city, a looming telecommunications tower houses the local turkey buzzards.[23] A friend of

---

21. White and Wilbert, *Technonatures*, 6.

22. Ibid.

23. I was reminded of this while reading the article by Steve Hinchliffe and Sarah Whatmore, "Living Cities: Toward a Politics of Conviviality," in *Technonatures*, 107.

my mother's at the local senior living complex remarks about the irony of how the residents watch the turkey vultures swoop on the air currents for their evening entertainment. The Big Sioux River also runs through the city, a mostly brown, agricultural river that carries a variety of species of fish and other animals. Humans and nonhumans cohabit the urban landscape, and the boundaries spill out from there. The boundaries of urban Sioux Falls recede into the surrounding bedroom communities, and the spillage of agricultural waste runs into the city waters of the Big Sioux. Raccoons cross from farms into suburban homes, finding their way from one garbage can to another. And acreages that were once family farms are now subdivided into urban landscapes of homes that seem to all look alike.

Cities are not simply urban, nor are farms simply agricultural. The maps and boundaries we have used to create those distinctions don't work anymore either. We seep into each other, becoming something new and different. This *becoming* of that which is new holds, on the one hand, possibilities and hope and, on the other hand, problems and despair. What becomes of our becoming will depend on how we negotiate these new landscapes, and even then the unpredictability of how we all get along together will change more quickly than we can imagine. That's why I cannot simply be church or be Christian with my old images and maps of both the city in which I live and the faith from which I come. Therefore, we must discover who we are as we become something new with the creatures and landscapes around us. Our vocation is not to simply baptize the status quo but to discover again and again what our place is in this world, and how can we make it more wholesome for all that inhabit it together. We need new theologies to negotiate and understand these landscapes that are becoming more and more complex each day. The boundaries between what is and what was are shifting, and so is our perspective. I have trouble figuring out where I am, where I should go, and what I should do. There are days when I walk through the neighborhood around me and scarcely comprehend where I am. That seems to have nothing to do with the direction dyslexia my husband accuses me of having. This is a kind of existential confusion, wondering about who my neighbors really are in a city and world whose boundaries are moving swiftly atop the tectonic ground beneath me. I simply accepted some relationships as having clear and firm boundaries: I am human, they are cows. You are a machine. I am not. This is rural, and that is urban. But I have discovered these bounded

Grounding Incarnation in Creation

relationships have imploded into something new which far exceeds the borders of my imaginative horizon.

I can think of no other event that has rekindled my imagination about my relationship to the natural world, other human beings, and technologies than the South Dakota floods of 2011. Here a disaster unfolded that didn't seem to obey the boundaries between natural and human. From where the Missouri River begins its natal journey at the headwaters in Three Forks, Montana, to the landscapes it carves in the Dakota plains, I watched and learned much more about the mighty river that summer than I ever did before. During the spring and summer of 2011, the mountain streams of southern Montana that form the Missouri River flooded the farms, homes, and businesses in the prairie landscapes of the Dakotas, Nebraska, and Iowa. Record snowpack in the mountains of Montana melted into the turbulent runoff that surges into the Jefferson, Madison, and Gallatin Rivers. That year these three rivers did not look like the clear, placid mountain streams that win blue ribbons for fly-fishing. Instead they tumbled forward and flooded over their banks of the Missouri River. All the state parks near the Three Forks were closed due to flooding. Fly-fishing was getting a very late start, and daredevil rafting an early and long seasonal run. The waters that give life to the valleys through which they flow are also the very waters that have destroyed life along the way.

But their destruction is not alone some so-called force of nature or some act of God. The Missouri River, once barely touched by the effects of humankind, now carves its path with the help of human dams, levees, and drainage systems. We, along with the forces of nature, are co-creating the depths of the river basins, measuring its flow on charts we decipher online, and fighting against its very torrents by frantically building large berms of white sandbags. Some of the areas down by Dock 44, near Platte, South Dakota, were submerged. These normally serene and beautiful areas, often painted by Sheila, are also favorites of mine. They waited, often like the oil on her canvases, until fall to dry out, and then we Midwesterners waited another year to see how once again the waters would rise and fall with the snows that melt, with the rains that come, and with the levees and dams we build. The mighty Missouri marks the threshold between drought and flood, creation and destruction, west and east, turbulence and placidness. We stand on the threshold: knowing how powerless we are over such a mighty river and yet how powerful we are when we can change the course of its tumultuous comings and goings.

65

The Geography of God's Incarnation

Norman Maclean made western rivers in Montana famous with his small novel, *A River Runs through It*. The story captures the adventure and rhythms of life of Montanans who combine their religion and fly-fishing into one spiritual experience. My mother reminds me that my grandfather was a good fly-fisherman who wandered up and down the banks of the Gallatin River. Many years after Maclean's book was popular, and Montana was becoming a more popular tourist destination, Hollywood produced the movie version of *A River Runs through It*. And sure enough, as the locals predicted, more tourists flocked to Montana. The location of the movie was changed from Maclean's native area near Missoula to the Gallatin River near Bozeman, the Yellowstone in Paradise Valley, near Livingston, and on the Boulder River near Big Timber, Montana. Not long after I saw the movie, I nearly bought a T-shirt that I found in a shop in Bozeman, which read simply "A Tourist Runs Through It." Tourists are one of the driving forces in the economy of western Montana, but some of the tourists who were rich stayed and bought the land. Public access to some of the best blue-ribbon trout fishing in the world was limited by those with power and privilege.[24] Many of the ranchers who I knew as a kid thought that their land was also public land, and they had the responsibility to share it with others. In a way, they exemplified a kind of responsible stewardship of the land. Over the last few decades, fighting over the "right of way" through these public and private lands has escalated into political wars. I remember testifying at a hearing in the 1970s about turning the lands up near the camp where I went every summer into a wilderness area. Charlie, my local prospector friend, thought that the national label of *wilderness* would draw more tourists and cause more damage to the land. I feared that if the land were not designated as into wilderness, the locals would not take care of the land. We were both right. The Absarokee-Beartooth Wilderness area no longer allows motorized vehicles, but it has become an area where lots of "tourists run through it." The local old McLeod bar, where chainsaws used to decorate the walls and where a lone jukebox was our weekend entertainment, has now become the Roadkill Café. I haven't stopped there yet.

Human intervention in the land changes the way that nonhumans live, reproduce, and thrive. Here are a few examples:

---

24. Montana Fish, Wildlife & Parks, "Access to Recreaton."

- "Reptiles and amphibians are at greater risk for vehicle accidents from off-road vehicles, and recreational activities can disrupt breeding habitat."
- "Human disturbance can destroy bird nests and cause adult birds to abandon nests."
- "Snowmobiles can crush small mammals that live under the snow, and snowmobile trails can make deep-snow areas more accessible to predators."
- "Destruction or disturbance of riparian habitat and use of motorized watercraft in waterways are significant threats to beaver and other semi-aquatic species."
- "Ungulates can be adversely affected if recreational building or activity disturbs their use of seasonal ranges."
- "While skunks and coyotes generally do well around human activity, grizzly bears and other large carnivores are at risk from the increasing year-round use of motorized vehicles in more remote area, which disturbs the quiet places these large predators need to reproduce."
- "Dogs accompanying recreationists chase, prey on, and carry disease to wildlife."
- "Human recreational activity can damage vegetation and cause other harm to sensitive habitats."[25]

No one should claim that we can "go back" to some kind of pristine, pure wilderness (as if there ever was such a place), anymore than we can "go back" to some kind of pure, pristine Garden of Eden (as if there ever was such a place). Such cultural and theological naiveté is dangerous. We are here and now, and can only move ahead. But how we do so is a theological and ethical concern. If we think that nature is only the backdrop for human activity, or if we claim that God only acts in human hearts, or when we separate non-human nature from human nature, we will misunderstand what it means to be created in the image of God. If we are created for relationship with ALL of the world, then we must reflect on, live with, and care about all of those with whom we are related. We are located in the connections between public and private, technology and nature, human and non-human. And God is in, with, and under these connections. But

25. Ibid.

the connections reveal how difficult it is to name who and where is God. For not all relationships or connections, at least immediately, appear to be wholesome or good. We must admit that suffering and tragedy mark our lives as much as goodness and joy. The creation, by the place it was created to be and by the place it has become, is ambiguous in its powers of life and death. In the book of Genesis, it is very clear that the word *perfect* is never used by God about God's creation. It is pronounced good, and even very good. But never perfect. We are yet to become that which we are fully called to be.[26] God not only created but also is creating still: the product and process are works in progress. Something is always coming out of nothing! Order is continually forming from chaos. However, we can't ignore the ways in which the very elements from which God creates and the ways in which creation is going are also troubling for our faith. No matter what the season, we know someone who is touched by some kind of natural disaster. Fire, water, rain, and wind destroy thousands of homes and lives each year. What are we to make of this? Can God be trusted? Can we be trusted with this earth?

Let's turn back to the two books about creation that we have used thus far to see what we can discern about these questions: the book of nature, interpreted in the epic of evolution, and the book of Scripture, interpreted within the traditions of Christianity. Together they might provide some clues to our questions.[27] From Genesis to the Psalms, God doesn't just create alone; God always creates the world in concert, in community, and gives others the power and presence to do the same, albeit in different ways. In chapter 1 of Genesis, God tells the earth to bring forth vegetation, and it does. "The earth brought forth vegetation; plants yielding seed of every kind, and tress of every kind bearing fruit with the seed in it. And God saw that it was good."[28] Evolutionary theory confirms that life has emerged through epochs, changes coming slowly and dramatically. And for life to happen, so does death. Terence Fretheim explains four modes of creating that God uses: "(1) God uses already-existing creatures as material for creating new creatures; (2) God invites nonhuman creatures to participate in creation; (3) God invites the di-

---

26. Here I offer the writings of Terence Fretheim, John Hick, Irenaeus, Philip Hefner, Arthur Peacocke, and others who understand that creation is an evolutionary and emergent phenomenon.

27. For my reflections in this section, I am indebted to the biblical hermeneutics of Terence Fretheim.

28. Genesis 1:12 (NRSV).

vine assembly to be co-participant in the creation of the human; (4) God gives to the human being an important role in further creating activity."[29] These modes of creativity are continuous with what we see emerging in the processes of evolution. Many Christians who read the two, the book of nature and the book of the Scriptures together, can trust that what is happening in the epic of evolution is in continuity with what Christians claim about how God creates the world. Creation is not a solo act, nor is it perfect the first time around. Instead, the world seems to emerge over time, with the ebb and flow of life and death, through mistakes, and is open ended. I recall again what I think it means to be created in the image of God: the vocation of the created order is to be and become freely that which fulfills God's gracious purposes and intentions for the creation. All creation is called to be creative, to join God in creating the world together in a concerted effort for a wholesome future together.

Creativity is our creaturely calling. Indeed, the elements necessary for the creative process seem to invite messiness, disorder, chaos, frustration, and even disaster. But from those elements come beauty, wholeness, adventure, order, and life.[30] I find myself aligning myself with those theologians from the early patristic era like St. Irenaeus to the contemporary theologians in the religion-and-science dialogue like Philip Hefner and Arthur Peacocke, who confirm what biblical scholars like Fretheim say about creation: that God is at work in the world, bringing forth something out of nothing and order out of chaos. However, the world isn't finished yet, and so there is risk for suffering and evil. Here I draw again upon Philip Hefner's language that human beings are created cocreators, coparticipants with God in bringing about the future of the creation. Some kinds of suffering are inevitable; they result from being created. We creatures know, all of us who are not God, that we are limited, finite, and mortal. While the rest of creation has been given the gift of freedom to create, humans bear special responsibility for their freedom they have been given. No other creature can cause such suffering to others. While the potential for natural evil has been present from the beginning of creation, moral evil seems to belong alone to human beings, but it is never completely separate from the natural world. We are all in this together in ways that can either save or destroy the world. Natural and moral evil

---

29. Fretheim, *Creation Untamed*, 19.
30. Ibid.

often coexist together in ways that are difficult to distinguish. The power of fire illustrates what I mean by this.

In his last book, posthumously published, Norman Maclean wrote about the 1949 Mann Gulch fire near Helena, Montana. *Young Men & Fire* is a drama about the power of fire and the lives of the young men who fight it. Fifteen firefighters, the elite Smokejumpers, dropped from the skies to fight a forest fire, and all but three died. Their story, told by Maclean, is framed by suffering and tragedy. Through the metaphors of life and death, and the pilgrimage he takes through their steps along the way to their death, Maclean extends the power of fire from the landscapes of Montana, but also to the mushroom clouds of nuclear power and fire. Maclean held a faculty appointment at the University of Chicago, and on the corner of the campus is a famous sculpture by Henry Moore to commemorate the first controlled nuclear reaction. Some think the sculpture looks like a human skull; others find a mushroom cloud within the smooth shape. Maclean finds both. Maclean wrote:

> The atomic mushroom has become for our age the outer symbol of the inner fear of the explosive power of the universe. It is the symbol of a whole age, and it took an artist to express the meaning the mushroom has for us. Henry Moore, one of our age's most expressive sculptors, commemorated the occasion that led to the Atomic Age—the first self-sustained nuclear reaction—on the site at the University of Chicago where it occurred. His bronze atomic mushroom, with its hollow eyes, is intentionally bi-visual from every point of view. Wherever you stand, the bronze looks like both an atomic mushroom and a skull, and it's meant to.[31]

Nobody understood this more than those who created the atomic bomb. In a haunting docudrama called *The Day after Trinity*, we are introduced to the story of how Robert Oppenheimer and other scientists and engineers worked together to create the atomic bomb in Los Alamos, New Mexico.[32] When they saw the purple clouds of mushroom smoke light up the desert sands of the basin called Jarnada del Muerto, they knew that the gadget had worked. Only a few days after July 16, 1945, when the bomb had been tested, it was dropped on the Japanese cities of Nagasaki and Hiroshima. The title of the film, *The Day after Trinity*, comes from the words of Robert Oppenheimer some twenty years

---

31. Maclean, *Young Men & Fire*, 295.
32. Else, *The Day after Trinity*.

later. "Robert Oppenheimer is asked for his thoughts on Senator Robert Kennedy's efforts to urge President Lyndon Johnson to initiate talks to stop the spread of nuclear weapons. 'It's 20 years too late,' Oppenheimer replies. After a pause he states, 'It should have been done the day after Trinity.'"[33] I show this video to at least one group of students every year, for the same reason, I believe, that Maclean wrote his book called *Young Men & Fire*: so that we don't forget how close life is to death, how close creativity is to annihilation. Langdon Gilkey wrote: "The unity of life and death in nature sets for humans their corresponding *spiritual* task of uniting life with death, our own living with our own dying."[34]

This last summer we went to the edges of Mann Gulch, where prairie meets mountains. And once again, this summer, forest fires are destroying thousands of acres of land, and we are asking young men and women to be dropped from the sky, to be saviors of a sort. What is interesting to me is Maclean's comment from the book as he remembers the way that the Ponderosa pines burst in those flames in the Mann Gulch fire: "The world then was more than ever theological, and the nuclear was never far off."[35] Maclean gets it: that God is in the connections between life and death, on the ragged edge, and so are we. Our vocation is to understand what those connections mean so that our future is not one of annihilation by fire but one of living into a wholesome and life-giving future with those to whom we are connected. We have been baptized into the waters of life, and with the fire of the Holy Spirit. Elements of creation, joined together with the promise of God's word, stand firm as a promise that God will bring life out of death, hope out of despair. Our faith is formed in the ecological, evolutionary elements of God's creative and redeeming work. More often than not, now these days, I am both in awe and completely baffled by it all.

I can think of no other place in my life where fire and water come together in more powerful and ambiguous ways than at Yellowstone National Park. The largest of the national parks, Yellowstone National Park was just ninety miles from my backdoor as I grew up; and as a kid I remember going there in early spring and fall to avoid all the tourists. In the summer of 1988, the land erupted in flames, though not from its volcanic landscape, but from several smaller forest fires that melded into

---

33. Ibid.
34. Gilkey, "Nature As the Image of God," 138.
35. Maclean, *Young Men & Fire*, 294.

one giant river of ash, smoke, flames, and heat. We were staying up in the park when it all began, and drove out that next day from our cabins at Canyon Village, with our headlights creating a pathway of light through the growing, heavy smoke and haze. In earlier years, people believed that fires were detrimental to the land, and so they were fought. However, the benefits of fires to the ecology of the area were later discovered, and so "let-burn" policies became the norm in many areas. But that summer, when drought had already taken a toll, the flames developed into firestorms, which swept through thousands of acres. Thousands of people were flown in to fight the fires. I remember worrying that my favorite landmark, Old Faithful Inn, might crash to the ground into ashes. Like the attempts to stem the flooding waters of the Missouri River, efforts to control the fires were at best difficult, and at times impossible. When we use language like "managing" and "controlling" these catastrophic natural events, we realize how powerful and unpredictable life really is. Where is God amid all this? For Maclean, and I think for me as well, God is somewhere in the fire, the water, the sky, and the tragedy of all of it. Somewhere in the death, new life comes. But in the transitions between, one makes a pilgrimage through all of it with prayers. Maclean wrote: "Dr. Hawkins, the physician who went in with the rescue crew the night the men were burned, told me that, after the bodies had fallen, most of them had risen again, taken a few steps and fallen again, this final time like pilgrims in prayer, facing the top of the hill, which on that slope is nearly east."[36] The year following the Yellowstone fire, 1989, my father died of a heart attack or stroke. We drove up to the park, where tucked amid the charred tree trunks, bright-green seedlings of new life were coming through the forest floor.

Because I love to escape from the chaos of my regular life, and retreat every year to the national parks, and in particular to Yellowstone National Park, I know that I'm tempted to think that like the Missouri River, where I've done some sailing, this is a place separate from the trappings of my technological and frenetic world. A recent article that I read about Alaskan tourists who visit the national parks said, "nearly every aspect of their Alaskan wilderness experienced is mediated by technology."[37] Of course I know this because now that I have cell-phone access in nearly every part of Yellowstone Park I realize that I can call home if there is any

---

36. Ibid., 300.
37. Clary, "Technonature: Wilderness and Simulation on the 'Last Frontier,'" 51.

Grounding Incarnation in Creation

emergency, and that I might be more easily found if I become lost while hiking. And I realize that Yellowstone Park is also a cultural icon of technonature. Every image that is marketed and sold by the national parks draws tourists to come and see nature. Yet, more often than not, what tourists like me will see are other tourists taking photographs of nature. I have taken pictures of tourists taking pictures of the grizzly mother and cub in the Hayden Valley. These are images of technonature.

Nowhere is technonature changing our lives more radically than at the intersection of the virtual and the real. The information superhighway, the mighty road of the Internet, has changed human communication almost as much as the printing press gave new life to the reformation of Martin Luther. Our social relationships have been changed by this threshold we cross every day into the reality we call virtual. Surely our gaze into the technomirror of the World Wide Web will call us to reimagine once again what it means to be created in the image of God.[38] Every day we are crossing a threshold from the real world to the cyberworld. This world of cyberspace challenges and reshapes our personal and social identities. In a recent book titled *Alone Together*, Sherry Turkle, a professor at MIT, explores these virtual landscapes, whose boundaries are shaped by the powers of the new social media. When we cross the threshold into cyberland, we move between the real and the virtual so that the boundaries between them remain fluid or even invisible. For some people, their virtual identity is more real than their real identity. Just think about the days when you descend into the world of Facebook or Twitter, where you intend to only spend a few minutes, and then emerge hours later, wondering where you've been and who you are.

I found out about Turkle's book a while ago when a former student of mine from Augustana College wrote to me on Facebook and told me that I must get a copy of *Alone Together*. Of course, if I were really technologically with it, I would have downloaded it onto my Kindle. (I do own one.) But for some odd reason, I wanted the real thing. I still wonder if those books that are stored on my Kindle are real. Do I love them as much as those that occupy the shelves in my library? In fact, why not just go for the virtual? As I chatted with this former student, we wondered if this language of virtual and real might also have something to do with being church, with trying to interpret what the real presence of Christ in the Eucharist might be. After all, this is about who we are as humans.

38. Hefner, *Technology and Human Becoming*.

The Geography of God's Incarnation

I wonder if someday people will rather prefer to go to virtual church. Maybe we will be taking communion online. It would be less messy, like those Facebook relationships we have with all our supposed several hundred friends. However, lest I pretend that these relationships aren't somehow real, I think about how many young people have committed suicide because their Facebook friends have harassed and hounded them. Their real identities have been shared by virtual friends in a very real world of shame and tragedy.

Sherry Turkle explains, "Anthropologist Victor Turner writes that we are most free to explore identity in places outside of our normal life routines, places that are in some way 'betwixt and between.' Turner calls them *liminal*, from the Latin word for 'threshold.' They are literally on the boundary of things."[39] I feel I'm at the betwixt and between my daily life: crossing thresholds between foreground and background, cyber and real, individual and community. The background is creeping into my foreground. I am crossing thresholds every time I enter Facebook or check e-mail on my Droid. Every time I cross the boundary between reality and virtual reality I wonder if it's worth it. What is it doing *to* and *with* me? Am I the same me online as I am before I go online?

Our computers, iPads, and smartphones are portals into the virtual world, but they are also portals inside our body-selves. Turkle says we are creating "life mixes" just as we create mashups. Our life is a mix of virtual and real.[40] You can be in more than one place at a time when you enter virtual reality. Turkle says, "When part of your life is lived in virtual places, it can be Second Life, a computer game, a social networking site, a vexed relationship develops between what is true and what is 'true here,' true in simulation."[41] In virtual time/space we can delay interactions and control them. In real time we cannot do that. How do we find our place in this wired world? Most of us will neither be able to nor want to give up the communication gadgets that connect us to our vast social systems. We have to learn how to live in this wired world in a way that frees us for genuine communication instead of in a way that holds us hostage to our gadgets. We may need to find other places, apart from the constant connections. Places to rest. And Sabbaths from the constant pressure to connect.

---

39. Turkle. *Alone Together*, 213.
40. Ibid., 161.
41. Ibid., 153.

I have also found that though they belong to a generation who often would rather die than give up their cell phones, younger folks are tiring of the constant demands of mobile devices. Someone is always texting, demanding their attention. I've even had to discourage students from reading messages in class. In at least one instance, these messages were suicide notes from a roommate, texted in class because the roommate knew that the other student couldn't leave the phone alone. This new generation is also seeking out other ways of connecting. In the *New York Times*, Pico Iyer writes about ways that we seek "the joy of quiet," and he claims that these times might possibly be the new luxury of the next generation. He states, "Writer friends of mine pay good money to get the Freedom software that enables them to disable (for up to eight hours) the very Internet connections that seemed so emancipating not long ago."[42] In fact, it is becoming the preference of the powerful to stay in luxury resorts for $2,285 a night simply to disconnect from the world. Furthermore, teenagers are now going to camps dedicated to recovery from social-media networks. Addiction has become a serious problem. Iyer reminds us that seeking quiet time is nothing new. He quotes Blaise Pascal, who remarked that "all of man's problems come from his inability to sit quietly in a room alone."[43] Many students now might long to be in a room of their own.

We also know that multitasking and doing too much in our wired world actually decreases our creativity and productivity. Iyer claims that "empathy, as well as deep thought, depends (as neuroscientists like Antonio Damasio have found) on neural process that are 'inherently slow.' The very ones our high-speed lives have little time for."[44] I had to laugh when I watched how many of us posted an article about seven things that "highly productive people do."[45] Almost all of them fell in line with Iyer's sentiments: we should slow down, stop multitasking, carry on conversations with people on the phone rather than by e-mail, and limit time online. I have both articles sitting in a folder on my desk. I hope that printing them out, reading them, and committing them to memory will help me create a different kind of space in my life: a quieter, slower, and yet more productive space. Crossing thresholds in this world is not easy.

---

42. Iyer, "The Joy of Quiet."
43. Ibid.
44. Ibid.
45. Pozin, "7 Things Highly Productive People Do."

The Geography of God's Incarnation

We remain both wanderers in cyberspace, tethered together in tenuous webs of relationships and also residents who long to be home in God. I believe our life reflects this tension, reflected in the images from Genesis.

To be at home with God we must find a way to be at home with ourselves and with one another. Will we find our home with God as a solo traveler, or will we find companions on the way? We must discover companions along the way—those who are flesh and blood, creatures like ourselves. Then and only then will we be able to see and understand what it means to be created in the image of God. To be created in the image of God is to be made for companionship and compassion. As Sittler reminds us, we are creatures, made by God to care for and enjoy the earth. We are earth creatures. My theological ancestors have known it all along, those who wrote the texts that shape my tradition, that the image of God is about relationships, our relationship with God and with all creation. We are created to be companions, critters together in the connections we make. But we cannot carry out our God-given vocation alone; to do so would be sin. The rest of the world, all that which is not us, not human, invites us to join, to be a part of God's ongoing creative activity. But we cannot do so with romanticized notions or with naïve understandings.

I have spoken way too little about the suffering and devastation that wrecks our life together. Every time I walk my dogs in the local park, I am aware that I go home to eat another animal for dinner. I make distinctions about which kind of animal I choose as a companion and which others I wear for clothes and from which others I reap benefits given their sacrifices in medical experiments. I sat with a friend the other night, and she reminisced about her interview for her first job as a parish pastor in Buffalo, South Dakota. Located on the intersections of Highways 20 and 85, in Harding County, the town boasts a whopping 380 people in approximately .6 square miles.[46] On a recent stop in the town, I noticed several trucks pulled up at the coffee and floral shop, Blossoms and Brew. My friend was interviewed by call committees from the town parish and the country parish. These groups wanted to know different things. Those from town wanted to know if my friend hunted, fished, or knew how to dress a deer. She fished but didn't hunt and didn't have any objections to others if they did. Those from the country parish wanted to know if my friend knew how to change a tire. The distance between the country and city parishes was approximately a hundred miles, and she would be

---

46. "Buffalo, South Dakota."

driving those miles with some frequency. Yes, she told them, she could change a tire. My friend was hired. She understood the geography, the economy, and the local cultures enough. What the call committee knew and appreciated about this outsider who would become their pastor was that she wasn't naïve about the place where they lived, and this was important. She eventually left Buffalo, South Dakota, and went on to do her doctoral studies in theological ethics, with a particular emphasis on Luther's understanding of vocation. We talked together about where our various paths had taken us in life. We are both native Montanans, have spent significant time in major metropolitan areas, and are now both employed as professors in a Midwestern city. We realized, as we talked into the evening hours, that the members of this call committee in Buffalo, South Dakota, were theologically smart. They knew where they lived and what they needed. And now, as the thundering roll of trucks from Highway 85 from the oil pipeline in North Dakota changes this small town on the prairies, they will hopefully ask again and again to those who come through their small town: Who are you? What about our future? And what can we do to live together into God's future that we share? We all need to be on call committees, asking what our vocation is as we live together—humans and nonhumans traversing the roads we share in this world we call God's creation.

5

Incarnation at the Crossroads

We Join Those Who Are Wayfaring Strangers, Along the Via Dolorosa, to the Forgotten and Wayside Places.

EXCURSUS

Crossing the Boundaries from Us to Them in the Gospel of Mark

*I*N THE GOSPEL OF *Mark, Jesus doesn't stay in one place very long. In the first chapter alone, Jesus is baptized in the river Jordan, is shoved into the wilderness by the Holy Spirit, and begins his public ministry in Galilee. One of Mark's favorite words is 'immediately.' Right now, directly and closely, in the moment, as soon as. Immediately. For almost fourteen chapters, Jesus is busy preaching, teaching, healing, and eating meals. Crowds surround and press in on him. In many of these encounters, Jesus crosses different kinds of geographical and cultural boundaries: from one country to another, from the clean to the unclean, from congested places to deserted ones, from the unfamiliar to the familiar, from his hometown to foreign places. In the middle of the gospel, in chapter 7, Jesus meets with the Pharisees and scribes who have come from Jerusalem to ask him about what it means to keep the traditions of the elders. The meetings, while not* *particularly friendly, seem to have an insider quality about them, of a Jew talking with other Jews. Jesus is inside familiar territory, even though others might perceive him as an outsider because he doesn't always follow the traditions the way they should have been followed.*

And then he takes a detour.[47] *He crosses from Jewish territory into Gentile lands. And on the way, Jesus meets up with those whom he might have considered to be his enemies. When Jesus crosses from his homeland into Gentile territory, he does not want to be noticed and he enters a house hoping that no one would find him there.*[48] *We don't know for sure, but Jesus possibly enters a Jewish house in order to find refuge in an alien region. And in this country, Jesus, a Jewish male, encounters a Greek woman, a Gentile. This story about Jesus's encounter with the Syrophoenician woman reveals the boundaries and borders that operate within the Gospel of Mark: insider/outsider, familiar/unknown, Jew/Gentile, male/female, clean/unclean, God/world. I think that most Christians would expect Jesus to be the one to cross the boundaries and welcome the stranger, especially the one who is his enemy. But it doesn't happen this way in this story. He is the one who hides out in a house, not wanting to be discovered in this foreigner's territory. In fact, the woman, of Syrophoenician origin, the stranger to Jesus, both challenges his prejudice and begs for his help to cast out a demon from her daughter. She is actually the insider, the one in her own territory, living in a region whose cities were powerful and wealthy. However, instead of healing her daughter, Jesus verbally abuses her, calling her a dog (the worst possible insult). What a wonder that she didn't slap him across the face!*[49] *Instead of returning insult for insult, she claims that even the "dogs" receive crumbs of bread. After this woman has stood up for herself, Jesus decides to heal her daughter but does so from a distance. I'm not even sure why Jesus decides to heal her daughter, but he does. He doesn't travel to her home but stays within the boundaries of the house he had entered earlier. He announces to the woman that the demon has left her daughter, and indeed she goes home to find her daughter lying on the bed. I think that in a strange way, in order for Jesus to heal the woman's daughter possessed by the demon, he must first be healed of his own prejudice and desire for seclusion from those he considered to be other. The woman of Syro-Phoenician origin turns out*

---

47. Mark 7: 34–30 (NRSV).
48. Swanson, *Provoking the Gospel of Mark*, 205.
49. Ibid., 208.

to be the one to teach Jesus a lesson about crossing boundaries to welcome the stranger!

After the demon is cast out, Jesus returns toward the Sea of Galilee, in the region of Decapolis. People bring to Jesus a man who is deaf and who also has a speech impediment, and they beg him to heal the man. As he touches him, Jesus looks up to heaven, sighs, and says to the man, "Ephaphatha." Be opened. While I don't know why Mark put this story right after the healing of the woman's daughter, I can't help but think that maybe Jesus also learned a lesson about what it means to be open and free, to be able to hear those whom he considers other. Maybe Mark is telling us that the people in our lives whom we find most foreign, around whom we feel the most uncomfortable, are actually the ones from whom we learn a great deal. Jesus had wanted to seclude himself from others, but he is challenged by this woman from Syro-Phoenicia. By her example, she teaches Jesus compassion and shows him a different way of dealing with boundaries of otherness. So, now, after returning from the region of Tyre, Jesus can once again heal others who, like him in a way, can become deaf and closed off to the humanity of those considered other. The detour to Tyre turns out to be a powerful lesson for Jesus on the way to Jerusalem. The boundaries we most often fear, because by crossing them we might meet and encounter those who are other than ourselves, can turn out to be places of grace. More often than not, they are places out of our way. Sometimes forgotten, sometimes empty—where God's presence can seem absent.

Where Deep Emptiness Can Spring Forth with Surprising Fullness

In the last chapter, we found ourselves within the cathedral of the cosmos, giving praise to God for our place within creation. We have traveled within our own locales, discovering the intricate, messy, and baffling connections between ourselves and all God's creatures. We have discovered that we are technosapiens residing in a technonatural landscape. When I'm on a journey, especially when I have a specific destination in mind, I can forget to look around me to see what is nearby and unnoticed, or to take the detours. When I reach a specific place, I must ask, what did I miss? Where would the road that I didn't take have led me? Who made the maps that I'm using? What place did not even get on the map? For now, we will leave the main roads, and cross thresholds into the empty places, the wayside and forgotten places. What we will discover there is what Christians often forget: that the Jesus way is not the main way, but the byway, the road that takes us to the nowheres and no-ones and discovers in them the love and grace of God. This is the *Via Dolorosa*, or the way of the cross.

Standing at the Borders, and Crossing Thresholds: From Nothing to Something, from Emptiness to Plentitude

Guilty as charged. I used to think of the Dakotas as the country one simply drove through to get to the really beautiful landscapes. When I first lived in the upper Great Plains, I did so as a freshman at Concordia College in Moorhead, Minnesota. I still remember the day when my parents' car pulled away, and I was standing by my dorm wondering why I had decided to move almost 800 miles from my home in Montana. While I would miss my parents and friends, I began to miss the mountains almost immediately. I felt like Beret, the female protagonist in *Giants in the Earth*, who left her home in Norway and moved to Dakota Territory. The vast grasslands and harsh climate nearly drove her mad. When I would look outward, I would think, "There's nothing to see." Flatland seemed to stretch everywhere and yet nowhere; cornfields and soybean fields dotted the horizon.

Almost fifteen years later I moved back to the Dakotas, this time as a professor in a small Lutheran college in Sioux Falls, South Dakota. Once again I found myself reading *Giants in the Earth*, wondering if I would go insane from looking at nothing. The prairie winds blew hot air all summer long, and in the winter I found it difficult to ski or be outdoors because as soon as it snowed, the snow was blown into crusted ice piles.

Then bit by bit we became acquainted with new friends whose love for the prairie challenged my notion that it was full of nothing. My husband and I began to walk the prairie landscapes with our friends, Janet and Ross. Ross is an environmental biologist and knows the names of every plant, bird, and tree. I learned about the mating dances of prairie chickens, about the oak stands in the Beaver Creek Nature Preserve, and how to listen for the multiple calls of cardinals. Naming the multiplicity and buzzing life forms on the Dakota prairies drew me into what I now see as a change of view. Nothing has become something. And that something has slowly become a perspective on the Dakotas that has me calling this landscape home. It's a different home than the mountains. But it has become one of the geographies that I now consider my dwelling place.

The Geography of God's Incarnation

Every year I make the crossing between the two landscapes that I love and consider home. When I depart on one of my pilgrimages back to Montana, I notice the changes happening in my body as I become alert to the signs of a changing scene. As the humidity levels begin to drop by Chamberlain, South Dakota, I anticipate the drier winds of West River. I will hear the meadowlark's song more frequently and will again be delightfully plagued by the magpies as their black-and-white bodies chase one another, diving to and fro. Between the farms of eastern South Dakota and the ranches of western South Dakota, the Missouri River marks the border between the two halves of my geographical and spiritual life. The first half, the relatively flat acres and acres of tall cornstalks and soybeans, shifts into the second half: rolling hills and buttes where wheat grows and cattle and sheep amble through miles of grassland. Fewer trees dot the horizon here, and clouds litter the dome of the skies. By the time I reach Wyoming, I know that soon I will see the Big Horn Mountains, with Cloud Peak in the distance. And finally I will cross the border from Wyoming into Montana. Occasionally, I see people stopping at the state line to have their picture taken, a memento of their journey westward. We must remember that all of us cross borders and come across boundaries in the regions of our life. How we cross them and what we do when we cross the borders in our lives make spiritual and religious experiences. Do some of us live within multiple landscapes, always crossing borderlines? Or do we only cling to one place with a familiar nostalgia, afraid to venture into new territories? Are some of us trapped by the place in which we live, not free to come and go? When we come to the threshold of the unfamiliar, which requires us to take a risk, do we simply retreat to a safe place within familiar territory?

The experience of crossing between two landscapes mirrors the spiritual and religious crossings we experience inside ourselves. Esther de Waal, an expert on Celtic Christian spirituality, lives and writes about her life on the border between England and Wales. In a charming little book titled *To Pause at the Threshold: Reflections on Living on the Border*, she reflects on the experience of living on the border between two different places:

> This book comes out of a particular place that I know, but it is ultimately about making any place or any circumstance the threshold into the other, the new, the strange, and showing the image of difference, mystery, otherness at work in God's world . . . The landscape, as David Jones reminds me, also points me to an awareness of movement, change, and ceaseless

transformation. If I were to sum it up very simply, I would say that it has made me aware of continual movement, crossing over thresholds while yet remaining firmly rooted in this place where I still belong. So at once I realize that I am in a situation that is not sheltered and safe, for to be transformed means being open, and while standing firmly in this place where I belong, I am firmly rooted yet never static.[1]

To be firmly rooted in the place we belong is to be open to that which will lead to our transformation. And some of us might be like Jesus, wanting to stay in the confines of a safe house, away from those who are other. But hopefully we will encounter guides, like the woman from Syro-Phoenicia, who will escort us, with grace, across the threshold into the other world. Once there, we must have both feet planted on the ground and yet always be ready to take a step into another place. At home and away: the history of the Christian tradition has reflected this movement between being rooted in one place and being on a pilgrimage. Settled, and simultaneously on the road. Christians belong to two worlds: the now and the not yet, where the reign of God is at hand and is not yet fully realized. We live *in medias res*, on earth as it is in heaven. We are citizens of both worlds. "To stand on the threshold is to be rooted, yet open."[2] I will always live at the threshold, between Montana and South Dakota. There is a certain restlessness that comes with this place between places. But I would rather live in the tension than give up on either place. I know that some people who find the places in which I live to be so desolate and empty that they don't even cross over, they simply fly over them. What do we find in the emptiness? In a poem that I quote below, I think a friend of mine has found a response. That in this emptiness, there is a fullness, maybe even the ground of our being, God, at home in that which seems empty. We might find our souls, our very hearts, in the places we have called empty.

Soul Shape[3]

> emptiness that is never vacant
> the sea's immense quilt

1. De Waal, *To Pause at the Threshold*, 12, 18.
2. Ibid., 27.
3. Hefner, "Soul Shape."

The Geography of God's Incarnation

never at rest
beat of the waves[4]
drumming like a heart
the firmness of a pulse
endlessness of the plains
brown paper stretching
wherever I look
wrapping the world
dotted sparsely[5]
with lonely night lights
blinking
from forlorn just
as lonely towns
and truck stops
open ready empty
the call of the mesas
breaking my heart
in the orange and purple
of day's end
land of the sipapu[6]
whence the first people[7]
wend their way
through

emptiness that is fullness
enchanting, some say—or
magical
depressing say others
bereft of green

you cannot plumb
the depths of this
emptiness—cannot know

---

4. Philip Hefner, Line 4—Are drawn from my two ocean voyages to Europe—10 days on the sea—and from the summers we rented a house on the beach on Washington Island, of the "thumb" of Wisconsin.

5. From Philip Hefner: Line 11—Are drawn from the many times I drove back and forth in college from Denver to Eastern Nebraska, especially the section between Grand Island and Denver.

6. From Philip Hefner: Sipapu in the myth of the Hopis is the hole through which humans emerged into the world.

7. From Philip Hefner: Line 23—Are drawn from the year we lived in Albuquerque and the trips back there over the years.

a beginning or an end
cannot reckon the beauty
holy, fearsome,
alluring
these nourish my soul
there's a starkness deep down there
that is nurture
if at bottom there is
divinity
God is spare
big bang power
galactic explosive
foundations shaking
even as they form
never fully shaped
shaking still
in the power whence they
come
dna-sprung
energy that lures all
moths to the flame
we were born of flame
to flame we are destined
febrile
labile
to flame we are destined
God is the fire
the shaking
the rumble
the whoosh
not much sentimentality there
but fire without end
birth everlasting
out of the
tremendum
that mothers
every living thing
light years of empty
infinity of
possible
endless poiesis[8]

---

8. *Poiesis* is a Greek idea of making and creating, the root of the word "poetry."

The Geography of God's Incarnation

When I first read this poem and let its words sink inside my memory, I recalled the famous painting by Edward Hopper titled *Nighthawk*. I count the experience of seeing it up close and personal in the Tate Modern in London as one of the most memorable of my life. It's a haunting piece of art. The loneliness shines from the late night diner's light; a couple stares away from each other. All we see of the other customer is his back to the world. The man behind the counter seems the most engaged; maybe he is thinking about the end of his shift so that he can head home to his family or his apartment. Nighthawks, as the name implies, are nocturnal birds, feeding mostly on insects. Notes from Jo, Hopper's wife, indicate that the name derived from the beakish nose of the man in the couple. I have always felt alone when I look at this painting, and I imagine entering the café, but there is no door, no entrance. The loneliness is palpable. Emptiness between the people. Late at night, maybe early into the morning hours, the couple and man sit apart. The cityscape on the canvas is powerful for me in odd ways, like the mountains or the emptiness of the plains can be. Even though I can be in the midst of millions of people, I can feel most alone. I have moved into the anonymity that a city can provide and also feel most at home within the swarms of people. My husband and I used to love shopping downtown Chicago on Black Friday, the day after Thanksgiving. We would ride the Jeffrey Express downtown and join the mobs of people, walking along as we looked at the newly decorated department-store windows. Cities are strange combinations of plentitude and emptiness, something and nothing. Sometimes the throbbing pulse of the city left me feeling alive, vibrant, and ecstatic. At other times I felt alone, surrounded by all, but connected to no one. It's not just the prairies in which people can find themselves alone and empty.

Now, in these Dakota plains, I have found something in the nothing; this has been a kind of spiritual genesis. Some people think I live in what they call the fly-over states. One day I typed in "fly over" into Google. Here's what I found in the urban dictionary: "States in the middle of the United States that generally aren't destinations for travelers or tourists and are generally flown over when traveling from coast to coast. Some fly-over states include Nebraska, Oklahoma, North Dakota, South Dakota, Wyoming, New Mexico, Iowa, and Arkansas." They are spaces that contain nothing or no one of any significance. They are not places, merely empty spaces. Another person reveals thoughts about where I live: "states in the middle of the country that are uncool and call

Incarnation at the Crossroads

soda 'pop.' *These* states have lots of farmland and stupid people and shit like that. They are called 'fly over states' because people never actually go to them and just fly over them to get from the east coast to the west coast. The square states."[9] I live in a rectangular state: in a landscape that we "fly over," that we "drive by," that we ignore. However, these landscapes can reveal a great deal more than we can see at first glance. I have walked through and driven along areas that some people consider to be simply a kind of emptiness or, worst yet, nothingness. Yet amid the emptiness is plentitude.

I used to drive or walk across the prairies and see nothing. Taking it in all at once, I ignored the details interwoven between the prairie grasses and the horizon line of sky and clouds. This view from nowhere seemed universally present; everything was nothing. In my own way, I was flying over the beauty of the land. But all my friends who grew up on the prairie seemed to love the prairie. At first I just felt sorry for them. They had never experienced real beauty like I had. This condescending perspective cast shadows on the relationships I had developed. I trusted my friends' views about everything else in life, so I realized that I must be missing something. While this may sound kind of hokey, I began to realize that the lenses with which my friends saw their world were kaleidoscopic. Like the perspective from a kaleidoscope, which at first is full of chaotic splotches of color and light, and then with a turn of the wrist, their view sharpened with patterns and shapes. The details sparkle with illumination. I realize that if I can't see the beauty in the place where I dwell, then I can't really see the beauty elsewhere (including in my home country of Montana). Now, on the horizon between earth and heaven, grass and sky, I see the yellow flashes of meadowlarks, the orange beak of the female cardinal, the tall, feathered switchgrasses, and the turning leaves of the bur oak tree. I know as well that in the farmhouses that dot the landscape families are struggling to earn a living from the carefully planted crops. Weathers of all kind threaten their livelihood. Emotions can unravel when the tornadic winds drop hail the size of softballs on corn nearly as high as an elephant's eye. This prairie, where nothing is clearly something, reveals both beauty and tragedy to the eye of the beholder.

This fly-over country is what I now call home, and since the mid 1800s, white settlers have called it the Great Plains. Joseph Bottum calls the Great Plains a wilderness. In some ways he is quite accurate: "Outside

---

9. "Fly-Over States."

lies the wilderness—not the manicured wilderness of postcarded rain forests and picturesque mountain peaks beloved by the designers of national parks, but the real thing. A cold that kills. Pestilence and blight. Plagues of locusts and blackbirds and dust. A summer heat that dries up on the stream beds and turns the high-banked cattle reservoirs into cracked-earth packets before they fall to dust and blow away."[10] Extremes of one kind or another shape the Great Plains, scorching heat and blowing snows, the current boom of oil and man camps to the bust of schools consolidating and the closing of Main Street businesses, a year of drought followed by two years of flooding rains, from nothing to too much. The irony now, with climate change, is that the earth is being washed away by floods, and the land is being exploited for economic purposes without enough thought and planning for the future.

In an essay about why he photographs the Great Plains, Michael Forsberg writes the following: "I have spent a good share of my time trying to make pretty pictures, because I think pretty pictures are important. They're particularly important here on the Great Plains, where most people on the outside looking in still think this holds nothing but flat land and a monoculture of corn, and where progress and value too often have been measured by how much can be extracted from the land rather than by the enduring value of the land itself."[11] In Genesis 1, God tells humans to fill the earth, subdue it, and have dominion over it. We have used this divine command to authorize exploitation of others and the land. I can't help but think that if we humans reflected upon the divine command to subdue and have dominion over the land in light of the command to love our neighbor as ourselves, we would do things differently. In light of recent ecological crises, some Christians interpret this passage to mean that we should be good stewards of the earth. But that word doesn't suit our relationship to the earth and all its inhabitants. When I think of being good stewards, I conjure up images of custodians and supervisors; we become guardians instead of intimate neighbors and kinfolk. So I'd like to return to Sittler's language, that we are neighbors, albeit ones with complicated and messy relationships with the earth, but neighbors nonetheless.

If we think of this vast wilderness as only a place to fly over, and not as the neighborhood in which we dwell, we will surely think that all the

---

10. Ibid.
11. Forsberg et al., *Great Plains*, 11.

neighbors, from the farmers to the species of prairie grasses, are dispensable. The vast grasslands in which many species lived and flourished simply disappear, acres at a time. Power lines, fences, invasive species, interstates, and rows of corn and soybeans abound. Ironically, those of us who live in these Great Plains might turn them into exactly what our coastal neighbors consider them to be: vast wastelands. We need to let others know that these lands are not ones simply to be flown over as if they are dispensable, but they are to be crossed through, lived in, and loved. They are our neighborhood, and simultaneously God's creation.

In the 1990s, stories about these vast prairie landscapes reached the *New York Times* best-seller list through the writing of Kathleen Norris. In her book titled *Dakota: A Spiritual Geography*, Norris returned to Lemmon, South Dakota, the land of her ancestors. She likened to a wilderness the country west of the Missouri, the stark, wide-open country surrounding Lemmon.[12] And so for a number of years, she made Dakota her physical and spiritual home. She also traveled to nearby monasteries, learning about the spirit of the land. I wonder what Norris would write about now as she thinks about this small prairie town called Lemmon, whose population, which had been shrinking, will be changing once again. This time it is growing. The North Dakota oil boom is creeping southward. People are moving into Lemmon, buying houses, and the town is preparing for what might be an explosion of sorts—of people and oil. In a prophetic and ironic statement, Norris writes: "The land does not change, or does so only slowly; maybe Dakotans emulate the land in that respect. The danger is that in so doing they can lose an important aspect of their humanity. In forsaking the ability to change, they diminish their capacity for hope."[13] Lemmon's neighbors, in nearby North Dakota, are migrating southward, this time at such a rapid pace that no one knows how to keep up.

North Dakota is changing rapidly, and the differences are waking up those of us who live south of the border. For months we have been hearing about the North Dakota oil boom. Boom times have come and gone in the Dakotas, and just as we did at other times, we all wonder what will happen this time. In contrast to what Norris wrote about in the early 1990s, at this time the land is being permanently altered, and so is the lifestyle of the Dakotans who live on it. For example, Watford City, North Dakota, whose population used to be around 1,500 is now around

---

12. Norris, *Dakota*, 3.
13. Ibid., 63.

8,000 and is expected to grow significantly.[14] From having no stoplights to several stoplights, the city is growing faster than it can keep up with itself. And Watford City is not alone. Just try to find a hotel room between Billings, Montana, and Fargo, North Dakota. No-vacancy signs abound. The new tenants have come to North Dakota from all parts of United States to find work during these tough economic times. And some of them are doing well, making at least $100,000 driving rigs on the open roads. Highway 85, that runs north to south through the Dakotas, is full of potholes, and the trucks create havoc everywhere they go. This North Dakota oil boom has brought great wealth to the state—so much that the leaders are trying to figure out how to spend it.

Not everyone is benefitting from this boom. The locals are besieged with skyrocketing prices for groceries and higher rent. Those who were smart or lucky enough to retain mineral rights to their lands are making thousands, while neighbors who long ago relinquished the rights are becoming jealous. And families who have come from out of town find the life in these North Dakota communities to be frustrating and difficult. Many of the employees are men. The wives and kids are left alone, trying to figure out how to make sense of the vast landscapes and crowded small towns, while also trying to make new friends. The "man camps" are sprouting up like weeds across the local prairies, choking out the local flora and fauna. Locals say that crime is rising. In a recent report on our local news station, I listened carefully to the following words: "The oil activity has pumped billions into the local economy and it's not done. Neither are the struggles that have come with growth."[15] I wonder whether we will heed this advice, and how South Dakota will cross this threshold of rapid growth in people, towns, and economies. The changes are right at our border—in the sounds of trucks crossing over Highway 85, in the houses being bought in small towns like Lemmon, and in the hearts of those who hope to become rich in these dire economic times.

The atmosphere in the Dakotas is ambiguous: hopeful for people who have found work, and fearful for those who don't know when the boom will go bust or what unknown problems lie ahead. One can feel the emotions of hope and fear that simultaneously shape the tone of almost every article and report about the Dakota oil booms. Local and national policies and procedures collide. For example, the process of extracting

---

14. Bartnick, "Boom."
15. Ibid.

the oil, known as fracking, highlights the tension between local and national, scientific and economic, agendas:

> The scientific and regulatory communities are trying to determine if the fear is justified. Meanwhile, it's become a political issue. If that spreads nationwide it could have a tremendous impact on what's going on in North Dakota. Yes, it is true that the Bakken fracking is for oil and not for natural gas. And yes, there have been no major fracking controversies in North Dakota so far. But if there were to be a nationwide moratorium on fracking—which has been discussed—the job and oil boom in North Dakota would go away virtually overnight. Put simply, there is no other way to profitably get the oil out of the ground. 'That (a moratorium) would shut it down, said Williston Mayor Ward Koeser, pausing and then adding: "Overnight."

While the fears of shutting down this process are understandable, so are the fears of those people who worry about what is happening to the environment and landscape of the Great Plains.[16] Nowhere is this tension more heated and noticeable than on reservations, where at least 10 to 15 percent of the oil exists. However, American Indian leaders have mixed reactions—reactions of hope for economic growth, and fear about the environmental impacts.[17] A quick economic boost could have devastating effects on future generations if everyone's vision is only nearsighted.

Surely now more than ever churches have an opportunity to take the lead in raising tough questions: Who will benefit from all this? What will lead to a wholesome future for all, not just for a wealthy few? Whose voices are being heard and whose are being ignored? Does the land itself have a voice? In the middle of an economic boom like this, everyone must ask, Who are our neighbors and are the neighbors' needs being met? I don't have immediate answers, but I strongly believe that these questions must be addressed, not only in the political realm, but also, and maybe most important, in the churches. Everyone involved must be alert to and protect the environment while also paying attention to the economic concerns whose needs are greatest. My fear is that what happened to American Indians, whose lands and livelihoods were destroyed decades before by greed, will again be left out of the decision making about their own lands. The ongoing genocide of American Indians by the Euro-American White culture is not finished. And the reason is that

---

16. Schactman, "To Frack or Not to Frack."
17 "Tribal Leader."

the peoples who have lived on the Great Plains for hundreds of years tie their destiny and spiritual future to the land itself. Genocide is also ecocide, large-scale destruction of the lands and nations by others who deem them dispensible.

When I was in junior high school, I remember hearing about the American Indian movement and its occupation of Wounded Knee. I had also read *Bury My Heart at Wounded Knee* by Dee Brown, published in 1971. Now, almost forty years later, I went to an art exhibition titled *Interpretations of Wounded Knee 1973 and 1890* at the Center for Western Studies at Augustana College.[18] Both Native American and non–Native American artists portrayed the slaughter of hundreds of American Indians by the seventh cavalry. A student had told me to look for one painting. I couldn't miss it. She was as deeply moved and disturbed by it as I was. The title of it is, *Still Hanging on the Res*. Nightmarish blues and blacks provide a background against which I immediately saw the steeple of a white church (which was at the site at Wounded Knee), pale bones of a skeleton, and finally what I didn't want to see: the figure of an American Indian male, crucified. I stood before the painting for a while, unable to move away from the power of the images. We continue to crucify Christ every day by not attending to the disparities and rights of all who are our neighbors, both human and nonhuman. Christians have always claimed that the cross is not the final word, that God's grace and love will prevail. But this painting reminded me that the very theology and church that I have loved is also, in part, to blame for the tragedy at Wounded Knee. Anytime that in the name of Christ, Christians withhold the grace and love of God, that Christians slaughter and abuse others in the name of Christ, the message of the gospel is nullified. Nothing and no one is simply dispensable, of no value. I hope that I never forget what happened at Wounded Knee and what still happens today all around me to those who are seen as simply dispensable. Anytime we see peoples and their lands as simply something to fly over, or view it all as a barren wasteland as we drive through on the highways, we will find it easy to ignore and exploit. We have to learn how to notice again, to see what is around us. If crucifixion means that we ignore and do not deal with our neighbors, then resurrection might mean that we listen closely and pay careful attention, so that we really get to know who our neighbors are.

---

18. See the Center for Western Studies Webpage: http://www.augie.edu/cws/.

I have known the names of some of my neighbors since I moved to where I currently live. However, I didn't know the closest neighbors to me, the names of any of the birds who come daily to the feeders. This spring I have been introduced to chickadees, the rose-breasted grosbeak, the downy woodpecker, and different varieties of finches. I realize how little I really know about the world around me. Joseph Sittler gets it right: "Contemporary humans are diminished because our roots are not as deep or as widely spread as were those of our forebears into the field, the forest, the woods. They do not touch the flowers, the animals, the daily tasks on the farm. Contemporary people, contemporary children particularly, think that hamburgers come from McDonalds. They think that Bordens makes milk and Kraft makes cheese. The closest any of them ever come to a lamb is a wool jacket. This increasing distance from the natural world has made our vocabulary bereft of natural images, has almost stripped us of the possibility to talk of ourselves in relation to God's creation."[19] If we are detached from and do not care about our relationship to the environment around us, particularly the lands on which we live, are we not also then detached from the Creator who made them?

Early in the colonization of the Great Plains, explorers found a diverse ecosystem, hundreds of different species thriving in the prairie landscape. Dan O'Brien, a writer and photographer, writes about how different the Missouri River Basin must have once looked compared to the drives he has recently taken through it: "Where Lewis and Clark had found elk, bison, wolves, and lots of prairie-chickens, I had found drained, black, cultivated fields where nothing was allowed to grow but corn and soybeans. I told them that the fever for ethanol was killing off the last of the biological diversity of the northeastern Great Plains."[20] I am concerned that so few young people I know have any direct relationship to the land. There is a movement underway akin to No Child Left Behind, called No Child Left Inside. Educators would learn about the outdoors, and be trained to take the country's children outside for their education.[21] Wouldn't it be wonderful if Christian churches started a complementary program? What if in the worlds of public education and the private sanctuaries of congregations, children learned to become environmentally literate? What if all our children learned about their landscape, the envi-

---

19. Delloff, *Gravity and Grace*, 14.
20. Ibid., 17.
21. Chesapeake Bay Foundation, "No Child Left Inside."

ronment around them, and not only learned about it, but learned to care about it and take care of it? The global neighborhood of the earth might have a future where all can have a wholesome life.

When I first moved to South Dakota, I didn't really care about the state or to some extent its people. I could only think of how long it took to get through it until I could reach the border of Montana. However, over the last few years, I have driven and walked through more of this state than have many of its natives. Recently I headed again to the Little Bend Recreation Area near Pierre, and then I drove for miles to the northwest tip to Buffalo, and Bison, South Dakota. (Little Bend is a spiritual sanctuary for me, a place where I can breathe deeply and listen.) Pheasants and meadowlarks were much more abundant than human beings. The quiet was interrupted only by the movement of water. As I looked outward, across the Missouri horizon of sky and water, I realize how much farther my gaze must reach if I am to grasp what God has created in this place. I must attend to the isolated and forgotten places, those along the wayside.

Wayside Markers: To the Small Places, the Forgotten Places

> A sacred place is a place where we are brought to the edge of our lives, a place that brings us into contact with transcendent values, with powers beyond our control. It may be a place of death or birth, a place of discovery or despair. The Celtic tradition calls these "thin places"—places where the gulf between God and us is narrowed. In these thin places we begin to see the hidden presence of God more clearly. The place-sensitive person is alert to the potential "thinness" of every place. The dingy, neglected, forgotten places: the ordinary, run-of-the-mill places; the carefully tended, pleasing places can all be gateways of encounter with God. They have a permeable character allowing the presence of God to be experienced through them.[22]

It's true that you "have to see it to believe it." Or in other words, to step into this place is to step into the stories it tells. A few months ago, I drove to the golf course in Canton, South Dakota. On the Hiawatha Golf Club is a small cemetery that belonged to the Hiawatha Asylum for Insane Indians.[23] I've read a lot about this place but still had not been to

---

22. Hamma, *Landscapes of the Soul*, 38.

23 Photos by Ann Pederson in 2010 and available for viewing online: http://www.flickr.com/photos/speakingoffaith/5301366736/.

the site. It's not easy to find. Surrounded by a split-rail fence is a large grave marker with the names of dozens of American Indians who died at the asylum. There are 121 bodies buried in the graveyard, in the middle of a golf course, on the outskirts of Canton, which is the seat of Lincoln County. In 1899, a local US senator, Richard Pettigrew, brought the federal funds to start this institution. A large, historic district in Sioux Falls is named after Pettigrew. When the newly developing field of eugenics was coming of age, many people in the United States believed that one way to rid the country of "troublesome Indians" was to claim that they were insane and could be sent to the asylum. Hundreds of American Indians from around the US were sent to the Canton asylum.

The Hiawatha Asylum for Insane Indians was intended to be a hospital dedicated solely to the "mental illness problem" among Native Americans. What it became was a kind of warehouse for storing "problem" Indians. When the asylum was visited in its later years, the following was noted in a report from Minnesota Public Radio: "The Indian affairs commissioner under President Roosevelt called reports of the asylum reminiscent of the terrible indictments Charles Dickens leveled against English poorhouses and schools."[24] More information about the asylum's operations came from the writings of Dr. Samuel Silk, the clinical director of the country's premier psychiatric hospital, St. Elizabeth's in Washington DC. He wrote that children were abused; adults were secluded in isolation for years. The asylum did not even meet minimum standards of care.

On the fairway between the third and fourth holes on this golf course, I wondered how my ancestors (Norwegian Lutherans) could live nearby and not know what happened to all these people at the asylum. Good Norwegian Lutherans. A good South Dakota senator. A history that is painful, ominous, and only thirty miles or so from where I live. Where do I walk today—in these times that I don't want to know about? That I turn a blind eye to? Shame won't do me any good. But a guilt that is confessed, that motivates me to tell this story might help me to do something about all those whose lives are hidden, not made visible, covered by those in power who don't want to know.

Who we are is where we are. Or at least where we have been and where we are going. I think about time. When? How long? I have been thinking a lot about the boundaries, borders, situations, dimensions and locations of our lives. When and where are interrelated. When and where

24 Stawicki, "A Haunting Legacy."

The Geography of God's Incarnation

is a complicated plot between local and global, then and now, over and under. What are the maps we take through these journeys? What are the cartographies of our culture? What are the maps that bypass the underground places? Why do I always drive by those little historical markers along the road? What am I missing in those stories?

When I first taught the Gospel of Mark with my colleague Richard Swanson at Augustana College, I realized how much I had missed in the narrative. His specialty is the Gospel of Mark, and he works with a troupe of actors, mostly college students, to perform and interpret the stories. What I forget, as do so many Christians, is that our gospels were first oral accounts, maybe shared around a campfire and told from community to community. Yet when we modern Christians interpret Scripture, we often forget this, and so we simply quote the gospels verse by verse without a context. When I read a play by Henrik Ibsen, I only sort of get it. When I see the play performed, I hear and see it in different ways. This is the same reason that Swanson's acting troupe reenacts the gospels, so that we hear, see, and interpret them in a whole new light. Consequently, when I teach the gospels now, I treat them first as stories to be told. Each of the four Gospels has something unique to say, and when we listen carefully, we might hear or see something new that we had missed beforehand. I have a vivid reminder of this when the Syro-Phoenician woman slaps Jesus, in the scene I wrote about from Mark 7:24–30. The text doesn't literally say that she slapped Jesus. But I saw the performance of this text, done from many different viewpoints. In one of these, the woman is offended by Jesus's calling her a dog, and she slaps him across the face. I had always heard the offense buried beneath the text, but I had never observed it. Through its performance this text came to life, and I was made to reinterpret this story within the Gospel of Mark as a whole. I had missed something in my previous hearings of this story: the offense.

I wonder about the offense buried in another story; this time the characters are not in a gospel of the Christian Scriptures but written on a historical marker in the center of Sioux Falls. I have walked by this marker again and again, scanning the brief story about an American Indian woman called Lost Bird. I knew she had attended school at All Saints, an Episcopalian boarding school, where the marker is placed.[25] I remembered something about Wounded Knee and that her remains had been repatriated and buried there in the early 1990s. A few days later, I

---

25. All Saints is now a senior residential living complex.

drove by the historical marker again and wondered how much more of her story I had failed to notice. After a few searches on Google, I realized the tragedy that occurred between the few lines written about her brief life. Lost Bird, whose name came later, was literally a curio for General Leonard Colby, who adopted her after she was found under the frozen body of her mother at the massacre of Wounded Knee.[26] The soldiers went to bury the bodies in a mass grave, and then they heard the cry of a baby nearby and discovered this small baby clinging to her mother. After she had been passed around from soldier to solider, Colby took her home to his unsuspecting wife, and she was raised in their home. Clara Colby, a rather famous suffragist, loved the little girl and raised her as she would have a child of her own. However, the story takes many tragic turns. General Colby had an affair and married his mistress, leaving Clara and Lost Bird to fend on their own. Lost Bird experienced racism and possibly sexual abuse, and was eventually sent to a reformatory school in Nebraska after she became pregnant. At the Milford Industrial Home, she was sent to spend time in the attic, the place of solitary confinement for those who couldn't obey the rules. After a year in the Milford Home, she returned to her mother and eventually left for Southern California, where she acted in the Buffalo Bill's Wild West show and in other bit parts. She eventually married and then contracted syphilis from her husband. "Eventually, Lost Bird and her husband gave up vaudeville and moved in with his parents in Hanford, California, in 1918. Lost Bird fell ill on Feb. 9, 1920, as an influenza epidemic swept across the nation. On Feb. 14, Valentine's Day, she died."[27] There is much more to tell. Some of it is written in a book about her life, and some is on websites and in journals. I know there is a great deal more to tell, not only from Lost Bird, but from other Native Americans whose lives were destroyed by poverty and racism. But this isn't the end of her story. There is also hope and more to tell.

In a recent conversation with a colleague who grew up on the Cheyenne Indian Reservation in South Dakota I learned about how Native Americans get tired of only being known as those poor Indians who grew up in such poverty and live such tragic lives. In a recent ABC documentary, Diane Sawyer went to the Pine Ridge Reservation to film *A Hidden America: Children of the Plains*. While the report did much to once again raise awareness about the children, who live in one of the poorest areas in

26. "Eventually, this living souvenir of Wounded Knee ended up in the hands of a National Guard general," in "Lost Bird Story Summary."

27. Ibid.

The Geography of God's Incarnation

the United States, it also once again reinforced stereotypes about Native Americans today. In reaction to this video, a group of teenagers created a rebuttal to Sawyer's show: a YouTube video titled *More Than That*.[28] "We have so much more than poverty," they tell the world! And what unfolds is a mosaic of youth who show and tell the world that they are more than the stereotypes which others impose on them. I am one of the "others" who have been taught the stereotypes and I want to learn the story that they are telling me: "we are all more than that." No doubt I missed that same message as I have read and learned the story of Lost Bird. She's more than that. She was a survivor, a mother, an actress, and someone who survived despite the odds. The least, the lost, and the last. They are people whose lives are more than that, more than death, they tell the stories about hope, survival, and grace.

On one of our random evening drives, on dirt roads, passing farms, and going by the Tea/Ellis corner, we took a road that was going north/south and saw a little cemetery with a historical marker. The words "Foster children" caught my eye and we pulled to the side. Nearby is a sign for the Bethel Cemetery. The historical marker about the Foster Children says:

> Robert and Lillie settled into a little sod house about 3 miles northwest of this marker. Six of their 9 children shared the primitive home. Within months, 2 of them perished in a savage storm. The winter morning of January 7, 1873, was unusually warm and Robert Jr., 14, and Sara, 12, left their home, lightly dressed, to go check on fox traps 1/2 mile north of their home. While they were out a blizzard hit without warning and disorientated them. They got lost and wandered 2 miles from their home. They came upon an old sod shanty while the blizzard went on for three days. People spent weeks after trying to find the children. A neighbor told her husband of a dream she had that the children would be found and he immediately located them. The children were first buried on the family farm and then moved to Bethel Cemetery.[29]

The blizzard itself becomes a main character in the story, wiping out the lives of two young children. The graves out in the Bethel Cemetery stand as sentinels over the bodies of many who lost their lives on

---

28. John Whirlwind Soldier, director. *More Than That*. Video featuring students of the Sioux Reservation's county high school. Online: http://www.youtube.com/watch?v=FhribaNXr7A/.

29 "Foster Children Tragedy."

the harsh Dakota prairieland. The cemeteries in Sioux Falls are crowded with tombstones and markers, remains of people's stories. Family members and friends place flowers and other memorabilia at the gravesites. I wonder who comes to the Foster Children's tombs to remember them. Cemeteries are thresholds, places between the living and the dead where we cross over and remember that we are dust and that to dust we shall return. I hope, however, that we are more than that. And that someday we will gather with all of those who are lost, forgotten, along the way and hear their stories to help us remember.

I wonder how I'd feel if those who manage the cemetery in my hometown decided to put a McDonald's right in the middle of it, or if they wanted to dig up the bodies and sell parts of them for souvenirs to local tourists. *Outrage, indignation*, and *disgust* might be a few of the words that would come to mind. And yet I think of all the places where commercial exploitation conquers the burial grounds of indigenous peoples. Close to Sioux Falls, South Dakota, is the Blood Run Historic Landmark, which overlooks a wooded river area. In close proximity are commercial and residential developments that encroach on this beautiful spot. This site belonged to many different Native nations for hundreds of years, and it includes burial mounds. There has been a move afoot to create a state park or national monument to honor the original inhabitants of this area. On the South Dakota Parks and Wildlife Foundation website are these remarks: "The opportunity to preserve a vital piece of Native American history is unmatched. But pressure to develop the site for homes and businesses increase each year."[30] And now, in this last year, the government has agreed to turn this land into a state park. The testimony of Allison Adelle Hedge Coke, a Native American author, educator, and activist, wrote poetry that was read at hearings for setting aside this land. Her poetry, in a volume titled *Blood Run: Free Verse Play*, helps to give the land of Blood Run, and those who inhabit it now and have in the past, a voice to speak on its behalf. The area set aside is only a fraction of what was once a bustling intersection of trade, commerce, and ritual. Gradually as the European colonizers encroached on the land, the native peoples died from smallpox, and the area was eventually plowed up for farming and later for other economic development. Hundreds of burial mounds now considered important archeological sites have been drastically reduced and desecrated. Buried beneath these mounds are the remains of a great culture whose history is

---

30. "The Blood Run Native American Historical Site."

The Geography of God's Incarnation

being erased. I hope that the memories of these mound-dwellers will be not only preserved in the historical markers in another state park, but also told and retold in the history books of the upper Great Plains. Whether it's the struggle about where to locate a mosque near the site of 9/11 or the return of the ancestral lands of the Black Hills to the American Indians, I must always remember that commercialization and exploitation often go hand in hand. The American culture is one that is driven, on the move. I grew up with ancestors who headed west. For good or for ill, I still haven't wanted to stop that love of being on the move, of driving through the wide open places that call me westward.

I have traveled all over the great prairies of the Dakotas and feel like I've discovered only a little bit. When I first got married, I told my husband, who was from South Dakota, that hell would freeze over before I would move to South Dakota and live there any length of time. I'm sure it is quite cold now in hell. I have lived in South Dakota for over twenty years and have traveled through much of it. We usually head along Interstate 90, where moving at seventy-five miles an hour, the borders between eastern and western South Dakota seem to be just a few hours apart. Along this familiar highway pilgrimage, we stop at a large outfitter's store, the shopping shrine for those who love to be in the outdoors. And at Al's Oasis we join fellow travelers, pausing at the threshold between East and West River. The Missouri divides the Dakotas in half, and the landscape between farming and ranching country also shapes the cultures and politics of the two sides of the states. Along the way, we always notice those same signs calling us to come and stop at Wall Drug. The signs are relentless and dot the interstates for hundreds of miles. The small drug store, started by the Husteads in the 1930s, became famous when signs appeared through the dry, hot plains that free ice water was just ahead at Wall Drug. Whether one considers it to be the tackiest tourist destination in the United States or the greatest place to stop for coffee and doughnuts, it continues to attract upwards of two million visitors a year. We are always among those who wander through the kitschy souvenirs and look at the jackalope statues, along our way to the Black Hills.

However, sometimes when we head to the Black Hills for some time away, we avoid the interstate and take the secondary roads. Highway 44, which is also referred to as the "South Dakota High Road" in the transportation industry, is "the only highway that traverses the entire state

Incarnation at the Crossroads

without a single overhead obstruction (excluding power lines)."[31] The highway covers some of the most beautiful country in the upper Midwest. We love the view from the Platte-Winner Bridge, where we have watched breathtaking sunsets on the Missouri. From there the highway creeps through the colored layers of rock and dirt in the Badlands. We stopped once at Interior, South Dakota, an entry point into the Badlands. Some believe that it's the gateway to the West. Tim Murphy, in an article about road trips through the United States, wrote the following: "Mostly, I'd say Interior marks the beginning of the West because of the sign, across the street from the church and the old jail, which sketches the town's vast narrative arc like a B-side from Herodotus. It may as well be a welcome sign to the West. 'The post office burnt down, about five years ago. When was that, it was five years ago? Yeah,' says Heather Tucker, manning the register at Badlands grocery store. 'That was pretty much the highlight of the last 10 years.'"[32] I don't remember much about the town; as far as buildings go, there aren't many there. But I do remember the isolation, the almost lunar-like landscape of the Badlands in its shadow. If this is the gateway to the West, which indeed it might be, it's a very different entrance than the one we always encounter at Wall Drug, the other entrance to the Badlands.

Sometimes when we head back from the Black Hills, we have taken other side roads. We pass through Wounded Knee, Potato Creek, up through Wanblee. Russell Means, a famous American Indian activist, actor, and member of the American Indian Movement, was born in Wanblee. That's part of the problem; we usually just pass through and don't stay. We really have grown to dislike the interstate, lots of construction, too much traffic, and surely not a way to see the landscapes we love. But they are ways to move, and in many cases have been set up to bypass sections of the state that are not as popular . . . the small rural areas where Native Americans and whites share poverty, heat, and long distances to services like hospitals and schools. Distance alone is a health-care hazard. Certain places in the world create health risks for those who live here.[33] Simply by living in certain geographical areas can mean that you are at greater risk for health related problems. There are academic disciplines devoted to cartographies of illness: about property,

---

31. "South Dakota Highway 44."
32. Murphy, "Where the West Begins (or Doesn't)."
33. De Blij, *The Power of Place*, ix.

purity, boundaries, frontiers, institutions, power, and definitions of place. Lots of people know about the maps of the human genome. Few people know about the high rates of cervical cancer on reservations in South Dakota. Initial results conducted by a team of researchers in South Dakota found that American Indian women living on reservations have a higher incidence of HPV infection. The background for the research explained that "high-risk strains of human papillomavirus (HPV) cause cervical cancer. American Indian women in the Northern Plains of the U.S. have significantly higher incidence and mortality rates for cervical cancer than White women in the same geographical area."[34] It's simply hazardous to one's health to live in certain areas of the world. And many cannot escape from their homes, but as they live in their homeland, must bear the consequences that others have created for them.

On the long drive from Hot Springs up through Sturgis, South Dakota (mostly on 385), we headed to Bear Butte. It's an abrupt mountain that rises up from the prairie grasses and was used for centuries by American Indians for vision quests and is still a sacred site today. We sat for a while, in 97-degree heat with a breeze, on a picnic table and listened. The flags on the visitor's center flapped in the wind, turkey vultures swooped around us, and storm clouds gathered on the horizon. That site was probably the highlight of the trip for us. While we do not come from a Native background, we could sense how powerful the place is and was. On the summit side of Highway 34, a small herd of buffalo roam the grasses. The features of Bear Butte are similar to those of the Black Hills and nearby Devil's Tower. In the long, hot days of August, thousands of bikers head to Sturgis for a rally. The quiet of Bear Butte stands guard against the chaos of the rally. From the problems of human trafficking to the shootings between gangs, the sacred land of Bear Butte stands in sharp contrast to these events. Amid the places that attract millions on the main thoroughfares, we need to uphold and cherish the quiet ones, like Bear Butte, that help us keep peace, a kind of sacred wilderness. The Scriptures give us visions of such places—places set aside for those who were in no hurry along the way.

The Gospel of Mark captures the tension of the busy, urgent business of the world of Jesus and holds it alongside his need for quiet and solitude. In the Gospel of Mark, Jesus is in a hurry, so it seems. As I noted earlier, the word *immediately* is used several times in Mark, reminding us

---

34. Schmidt-Grimminger et al., "HPV Infection," 11.

of the urgency of Jesus' mission. Jesus announces that the time is fulfilled and that the reign of God is near. The rule of God has both spatial and temporal dimensions—just not in the way that one would have expected them to be. "While the kingdom is not to be found in a particular place, it comes in the new state of human affairs where the values of the world are reversed."[35] Jesus found the kingdom among all the people whom we met that others had cast by the wayside, the lepers, tax collectors, the prostitutes, and those possessed by demons. In the places and with the peoples we least expect, Jesus comes and brings the reign of God. The Jesus way is not the main highway to God, but the way that makes a way out of those who have had no way.[36]

After healing people, eating with sinners, and casting out demons, Jesus would head out in the early morning, while it was still dark, to a deserted place and pray. No doubt his disciples, frustrated that they couldn't find him, reminded him that the message must be proclaimed. In fact, it seems that the more Jesus preached and ministered to those who were considered the least and last in his culture, the more he needed to find those deserted places where he could rest and be restored by prayer. In the Gospel of Mark, Jesus appears to be more and more exhausted, even growing frustrated and angry with the disciples. Before he faces the torture of the cross and his fear of being abandoned by God, Jesus retreats to a garden with his disciples to pray. We all need those places set apart, where we can withdraw amid the chaos of the world.

I think that to be in the places where those in the world suffer and are lost, we must travel to and remain awhile in those vulnerable places in our own lives. For many people these landscapes can bear the trauma and vulnerability of their past. Beldan Lane wrote about these places that carry within them a certain kind of woundedness: "Some wounds—we are grateful to confess—never heal. They grow with us, festering and prodding, reminding us often that the wound is what grants the storyteller his narrative power. Most people, I suspect, can plot a geography of broken places in their lives, pointing to fierce landscapes and threatening terrain they have negotiated alone or with others. Their wound even becomes, sometimes, an anchorage."[37] For me, one of those wounds comes

---

35. Hamma, *Landscapes of the Soul*, 82.
36. Coleman, *Making a Way Out of No Way*.
37. Lane, *Landscapes of the Sacred*, ix.

when I think about the experiences my ancestors went through when they immigrated to the United States from Europe.

We link our ancestors to the places from which we have come. My ancestors on my mother's side came from Norway and Sweden, immigrants to Minnesota, North Dakota, and eventually Montana. On my father's side, they were from Scotland and Ireland and immigrated to the United States in the late 1700s and early 1800s to Pennsylvania. They brought their homelands with them through the customs they practiced and the stories they told. However, as many of us know, there were stories that were never told, and even those get passed on to the next generations without words. These immigrants crossed thresholds from the lands they left to the new ones. No longer from the old country, not yet fully established in their new home, they struggled with their identity. When I first read Ole Rolvaag's trilogy about these immigrants, I understood more about myself and my own spiritual landscape. The stories move from the settling of the prairies by Beret and Per Hansa to the struggles of their children as they try to make sense of their parents' worlds and their new American identity. Like many today who immigrate to the United States and feel caught between two worlds, home is somewhere in between.

Michael Aune, a Lutheran historian and theologian, reflects on this immigrant spirituality.[38] He explains that many Americans were and still are hybrids, their identity marked by a hyphen. They were Norwegian-Americans, Irish-Americans, and Polish-Americans. Rolvaag knew well the dangers of the American temptation to make everyone the same, to blend everyone into the same bland stew or melting pot. Aune remarks: "He [Rolvaag] scorned the romantic notion of America as the great melting pot of nationalities, trying mightily to portray faithfully the cost of immigration as well as the gains, and believing the value of each distinct cultural contribution to our national life."[39] Beret, the female protagonist, nearly loses her mind as she longs for home in the old country while struggling to make a new home for her family. Her sanity hangs by a thread at one point during the epic prairie saga. However, she is the one character who endures; she never completely relinquishes her native identity, her mountains of Norway. She learns to live on the threshold, comfortable that by crossing over too far one way or the other she will lose her way. "What makes Rolvaag's Beret such a dynamic character is an integrating harmony

---

38. Aune, "Using the Fictions of Ole Rolvaag and Arturo Islas," 146–54.
39. Ibid., 147.

of religious faith and pragmatic realism that places her squarely in the present world of time and history and under the ever-present shadow of mortality."[40] Beret stood at the threshold of the frontiers of the West and the heritage of her homeland in Norway, between the new and the old, between self-reliance and roots in community.

Wandering is endemic to many of the Americans who immigrated. Many moved constantly westward, toward ever expanding horizons. However, finally many settle and make a home in their new world. "Perhaps Americans with no clear ethnic identity are even more likely to feel that they have lost their tether to the world, lost any sense of home, since American mobility makes allegiance of any sort, to community, to place, to history, a rarity."[41] Beret is the anchor of tradition, the one who finally settles and creates a home. Per Hansa, her husband, the one who is always on the move, wanders out one night in a blizzard, never to return. He dies facing the west. Left on her own, Beret raises her son, Peder Victorius. He carries within him the same desire of his father; he is always looking westward, outward, and is caught up with the pragmatic spirit of the American frontier. He crosses the threshold from his mother's and father's past into a new America. And with this crossing come others. In the third and final story, Peder falls in love with and marries Susie, an Irish Catholic. Neither family is happy about the marriage. Tensions build, and the novel ends tragically. As Per Hansa dies in the first book, facing westward, so the marriage between Susie and Peder dies: she leaves him, taking her son. She can't bear his tirades, and he can't understand her religion or family. The death is a divorce of love and families. At the end of this book, the reader is left with the echoes of Henrik Ibsen's *The Doll's House*.

Rolvaag, like the characters in his book, stood on the threshold, between the old and the new, between former identities and trying to create new ones. The boundary or border between the new world and home shapes the psychological and spiritual well-being of the immigrants of Rolvaag's world. Crossing thresholds. The spiritual dilemma of Rolvaag and his characters consists in coming to terms with leaving homeland and never finding a real home in the new land to which they immigrate. Homesickness and displacement are the theological and spiritual realities. We know them in our bones. Rolvaag's characters experience a loss

40. Ibid., 7.
41. Ibid., 152.

of a center, of a place to call home. And the land in which they live is harsh and often unforgiving. For Rolvaag, the land itself is a character, with subjectivity and power. The earth shapes and carves the characters of the story. The stories are tragic, and not particularly hopeful. They stand more as a warning about what Rolvaag feared would lie ahead in this new country: that on the one hand, diversity and difference when blended into a pot will melt into triviality of relativism; and on the other hand, when homogeneity rules, relationships disintegrate into violence. Loss happens either way.

For some people on the Dakota prairies, the vista is one of loss. They look out to the horizon, and their way of life as they knew it is vanishing. Joseph Bottum, in a review about the *The Children's Blizzard*, writes: "To visit that hard South Dakota country now, coming upon the little towns with their water towers, their white houses and cemeteries filled with upright headstones, is to see the price the homesteaders paid, for each of these towns was carved from the plains, grave by grave."[42] During these few months, I have driven by cemeteries, tucked under trees by a small dirt road. A few graves mark where families bury their dead. That is happening for different peoples in different ways.

A few years ago I taught a course called Living until We Die, Dying until We Live, about end-of-life issues. My coteacher was a palliative-care physician, and we spent much of the class reading and learning about the end of life from a spiritual and medical perspective. For the final projects, students had to present the results of a conversation they had had with someone who was either dying or elderly and nearing the end of life. One young man interviewed his grandmother, who lived in a small town in northern South Dakota. As he introduced his project, I wondered if this would be yet another sincere but typical presentation about how much he loved his grandmother and her views on the end of life. What happened was not at all what we expected. What emerged from yet another Powerpoint presentation startled us. He showed stark, haunting black-and-white photographs of his grandmother and the town in which she lived. Interspersed with the photographs were fragments of text, conversations he had with his grandmother about the loss she was experiencing. She spoke of how not only her life was ebbing away, but also the life of everything she knew around her. This small town was slowly dying as well. The schools had been consolidated and moved to another town, the church

---

42. Bottum, "The Cold, Hard Truth," D-10.

was losing members and would likely close, and many of her friends had died. Young people were not moving back, and the future of this small town and its way of life was like her life: slowly but surely ebbing away.

Some of the small prairie towns are dying. The oil boomtowns in North Dakota might be the current and volatile exception. In a 1991 article from the *New York Times*, over twenty years ago, the ebb and flow of small-town life on the prairies was being noticed: "Like giant tombstones marking the ghosts of commerce, most of the shops along Main Street now stand shuttered, as stark and still as the flat, unbroken plains of western Nebraska. The latest blow, and perhaps the most devastating, comes later this month, when the bank closes its doors. 'It's like dying a slow death,' said Dennis Edkahl, who has taught shop class at Venango High School for 24 years. Across the country, but especially in the Farm Belt, life is ebbing from the little towns that have long been revered as a cornerstone of American society."[43] The farm crisis of the 1980s devastated much of the upper Great Plains, but many other factors have contributed to the slow deaths of these communities. When interstates were built, many small towns were bypassed.

One small town that the railroads and highways have long passed by is Sharon, North Dakota, the birthplace of my mother. Visiting Sharon was one of these small pilgrimages that I took during sabbatical. I decided that I needed to see for myself where my mother grew up during the first years of her life. Located in Steele County, Sharon had a population in of ninety-six people in 2010, down from 109 in 2000. The town was founded in 1896. My mother's family moved there around 1920, and she was born in 1923. Her father was a building contractor. She remembers local stores, her Lutheran church, friends' houses, and the main street. The local telephone operator, whom they all called Auntie Harmon, most likely knew where everyone was. My mom recalls one such episode when her mother and several other women in the town began to wonder why their husbands weren't home. Later on that evening, the men were discovered in a local railroad car, playing cards and probably sharing a drink or two. The message that they were okay spread from Auntie Harmon back to the wives of the men.

What my husband and I saw in Sharon, North Dakota, was drastically different from the images my mother remembered. We drove out to the small cemetery, and there she found the gravesites of friends and family she had known. For six years my mother and her family stayed in

---

43. Johnson, "The Nation," A.2.

North Dakota, until 1929. That year, of course, everything changed. The Great Depression came, and with it came the loss of opportunities for her father's construction company. They packed up and headed west to Bozeman, Montana, where she spent most of her life. On what is left of the main street in Sharon is a faded billboard celebrating the town's centennial. The pictures that someone had painted of the town in its prime are now fading. I have no idea what will happen to Sharon, North Dakota. Most likely, someday soon the post office will be closed. That will be the end. I felt an odd sense of loss as we drove away from Sharon that day. I've never lived there, but I know that some part of my mother's life was shaped by the small Norwegian immigrant community that settled there. I do know that her story was much richer and yet also more painful than I will ever know.

Last summer I visited my mother's first cousin, a sprightly eighty-three-year-old woman, who had recently battled stomach cancer and yet bounded out of her front door to greet us. Before we had hardly spoken, we were both sorry we had not met sooner. She led us through her house. (Her belongings were being packed for a move.) Her husband, now recently deceased, had needed to be moved to an assisted-living center. At one point, on the house tour, she paused before a painting. In a small gold frame, I saw two hunting dogs in chase through prairie grasses. The painting was by my grandmother. I knew she had some artistic talent, but all of her artwork had been left behind by others or sold, and my mother and I had nothing of hers. Here was a memory of her talent, of her other life before she moved to Sharon, North Dakota. My cousin, in a gracious gesture, gave me the painting. I had it reframed, and it sits now near my fireplace. She was quite a good artist, and I have no idea how or where she developed that talent. I also know she had many other talents. She was a master gardener, a baker, and a friend. Earlier in her life, while she was growing up in western Wisconsin, something also happened to her that changed her life, and that I had come to know about only in my adult life. My grandmother had a child out of wedlock and was sent away to a place in St. Paul, Minnesota, to have the baby. That's what families did then—good, well-meaning Christian families, who sent the women away. My grandmother's child was eventually adopted into the family by distantly related cousins. I will never know how or why my grandmother became pregnant, but my mother recalls the grief and tears the incident would bring when mentioned. This is a story we know little about, but I know it is somewhere in my own bones and tissues, which connect me to her: my maternal grandmother, who died when I was two. She is only a memory to me but is not ever forgotten, and always loved.

Conclusion: From Nothing to Something

> I consider that the sufferings of this present time are not worth comparing with the glory about to be revealed to us. For the creation waits with eager longing for the revealing of the children of God; for the creation was subjected to futility, not of its own will but by the will of the one who subjected it, in hope that the creation itself will be set free from its bondage to decay and will obtain the freedom of the glory of the children of God. We know that the whole creation has been groaning in labour pains until now; and not only the creation, but we ourselves, who have the first fruits of the Spirit, groan inwardly while we wait for adoption, the redemption of our bodies. For in hope we were saved. Now hope that is seen is not hope. For who hopes for what is seen? But if we hope for what we do not see, we wait for it with patience ... What then are we to say about these things? If God is for us, who is against us? He who did not withhold his own Son, but gave him up for all of us, will he not with him also give us everything else? Who will bring any charge against God's elect? It is God who justifies. Who is to condemn? It is Christ Jesus, who died, yes, who was raised, who is at the right hand of God, who indeed intercedes for us. Who will separate us from the love of Christ? Will hardship, or distress, or persecution, or famine, or nakedness, or peril, or sword? As it is written, "For your sake we are being killed all day long; we are accounted as sheep to be slaughtered." No, in all these things we are more than conquerors through him who loved us. For I am convinced that neither death, nor life, nor angels, nor rulers, nor things present, nor things to come, nor powers, nor height, nor depth, nor anything else in all creation, will be able to separate us from the love of God in Christ Jesus our Lord.[44]

When I die, I want this passage from St. Paul's letter to the Romans to be read at my funeral. When I doubt my place in the world, when I feel dislocated and disoriented, these words (unlike any other in Scripture) alone give me a hopeful sense about my place in the world and God's place in my life. I can know that if God loves and saves all creation, then

---

44. Romans 8:31–39 (NRSV).

The Geography of God's Incarnation

surely God will also love and save me. St. Paul uses vivid imagery to give voice to the pains of our labor, to express our fear of being in bondage and our desperate longing for freedom, and to give us hope that we will find our place in the world, that is, to be at home in God and God at home in us. For everyone and everything who has had the experience of feeling they have no home, of being in exile from all that they love, of having no map to find their way, God's love and grace will give them hope of finding a home, a place in the world. The experiences of being displaced, replaced, or dislocated, while universal, vary in the personal details. The purpose of this chapter is to tell the stories of those who have been lost, left by the wayside, and forgotten; of those who have no place. The universal scope of God's grace is found in the particulars of our place. To put this in theological language, the incarnation and atonement tell me that in order for me to dwell in God, God must also dwell in me. How does this happen? By remembering where we have come from, we will know where we are, and where we are going.

As we reflected on our place in the universe in chapter 3, we know that the universe as depicted by modern science is dynamic, evolutionary, emergent, multileveled, and messy. This imagery is not so different from Paul's image of the body of Christ in his first letter to the Corinthians. In a sense, the body of Christ is a place, a community of relationships that locates our relationship to God and with one another. Being part of the body of God means that we are fully at home in the world, with ourselves, and with God. "We are not resident aliens in this world of God but fully naturalized citizens in our natural home."[45] Knowing that God is at home in us, and we in God, we experience the mutual indwelling of God and self. God dwells in us, and we dwell in God. In the language of the Eastern Orthodox tradition, *theosis* happens; God takes our place, and we are placed within God.

God takes God's home in us so that we are freed to enter into the places where others feel displaced, and dislocated. God adopts us as children, giving us a home within the family of God so that we can help others find their spots in the family of God. No one or nothing should be separated from the love of God. But that is not the experience for much of the world. We can't ignore the fact that many people in our world are displaced, that some areas are dangerous and sinister, and that our traditional road maps have only traced the main highways, ignoring the

---

45. Pederson, "The Juxtaposition of Naturalistic and Christian Faith," 122.

wayside markers and bypassing the forgotten and small places. One way that we can change the map of our theological tradition is to change the way we go, to find a new starting place, and to simply wander nearby and notice what's around us.

6

The Incarnational Marks of the Church
The Church Is Incarnational When It Is Universal, Apostolic, Sacramental, and Eschatological

EXCURSUS

Wisdom While Hiking over Columbine Pass

> "Accidents in the mountains are less common than in the lowlands, and these mountain mansions are decent, delightful, even divine, places to die in, compared with the doleful chambers of civilization. Few places in this world are more dangerous than home. Fear not, therefore, to try the mountain-passes. They will kill care, save you from deadly apathy, set you free, and call forth every faculty into vigorous, enthusiastic action. Even the sick should try these so-called dangerous passes, because for every unfortunate they kill, they cure a thousand."[1]

> "May God grant me to speak with judgment, and to have thoughts worthy of what I have received; for he is the guide even of wisdom and the corrector of the wise. For both we and our words are in his hand, as

---

1. Highland, *Meditations of John Muir*, 5.

The Incarnational Marks of the Church

are all understanding and skill in crafts. For it is he who gave me unerring knowledge of what exists, to know the structure of the world and the activity of the elements; the beginning and end and middle of times, the alternations of the solstices and the changes of the seasons, the cycles of the year and the constellations of the stars, the natures of animals and the tempers of wild animals, the powers of spirits and the thoughts of human beings, the varieties of plants and the virtues of roots; I learned both what is secret and what is manifest, for wisdom, the fashioner of all things, taught me."[2]

Part of my need to head west every year is that the places where I experienced the ragged edges of life (sometimes literally) were when I hiked up the mountain trails, up several thousand feet, sweating from the backpack full of supplies, to an alpine pass where the wind sculpted the trees into bent frames of knotty pine. Even the lodgepole pines begin to shrink and struggle at the edges of the timberline. With nothing but a pack on my back, no phone to call for help, and only blaze marks or cairns to make my way, I'm suddenly aware of my vulnerability. One wrong step and I could fall to my death, or one act of misjudgment and I could end up in dangerous situations where hypothermia and heat exhaustion occur almost simultaneously. But that never stopped me from hiking upward, to the place where I knew the view was unlike any other. For several summers I hiked up the trail about ten or eleven miles to Columbine Lake, and then on over Columbine Pass to Pentad Lake. Columbine Pass, famous for its array of alpine flowers, was the first pass I ever walked through, a threshold between mountain vistas. To even reach Columbine Lake in one day with a full pack was an accomplishment for me. While the trail was comparatively easy to others I had hiked, its eleven miles and gradual gain of three thousand feet of elevation was still a workout for me. For several summers, I led backpack groups up this trail and beyond through the forty mile loop across the lake plateau in the Absarokee Beartooth Wilderness Area. My favorite campsite was at Wounded Man Lake where I could see Chalice Peak in the distance.

One summer a group came from Minnesota, and I decided to take these eager high school students on an overnight to Columbine Lake. While the twenty-two-mile round-trip hike was a bit extreme for an overnight, they eagerly agreed and we set out on an early morning on a warm summer day in mid-July. We went on trips like this when accreditation and worry about litigation were still not part of the camp's guidelines for safety! I picked this trail because it moves slowly and graciously for those who are

2. Wisdom of Solomon 17:15–22 (NRSV).

not used to high altitudes. The first four miles crawl upwards through stands of lodgepole pines, and come to the East Fork of the Main Boulder where a rather larger bridge crosses the river as it flattens into deeper green and blue pools. The group of Minnesotans had adapted well to our pace and so we stopped to rest and have lunch. After trail sandwiches of rye krisp, peanut butter, and raisins, we proceeded on our way to Columbine Lake when we heard voices behind us. Soon a group of hikers from a university in Oregon were passing us by, on their way to Columbine Pass to study the flowers. No doubt we all noticed their calf muscles rippling against their shorts and hiking pants as they steamed past us on the trail!

Much later on that hot July afternoon, our group made a valiant effort and came over the ridge, down that final stretch of trail where it leveled off, and the view of blue water was just ahead. The lake, while small, is surrounded by the deep green of alpine meadows, dotted with melting snow from the previous winter. Indian paintbrush and elephant head flowers peeked up through the carpet of pine needles and occasional patches of green moss. After cooking dinner, and setting out our tarps for the night, we built a fire and relaxed into the evening sun. Over the horizon, and not long after a few laughs, we noticed clouds building and the wind picking up. I remember specifically checking with the students to make sure that they had adequate rain gear and was assured by all of them, and their group leader, that this was the case. They were ready for the timberline weather. By dark, a sudden mountain storm was upon us, with raging winds and pounding rains. From a flurry of packs coming undone, the kids and I grabbed our rain gear and tried to cover the sleeping area. But the ponchos and tarps were not enough protection for what appeared to be gales of rain. They were getting drenched, and some of the kids were already complaining about being cold and tired. I knew that hypothermia might not be far away. We had two choices: to stay and try to literally weather out the storm, risking hypothermia, or to hike back in the dark, risking two icy-cold creek crossings with only two flashlights. I'll never know if we made the right decision, but we opted for the latter.

I never told the group or anyone else for a number of years how scared I was about the hike back down the mountain that we made that night. We packed up our wet gear, and I led with one flashlight and put our strongest, tallest guy in the back with the other flashlight. About three miles down the trail we came to the first creek. In the dark, with waters rising from the rain, we loosened pack straps and faced the crossing together. We placed the bigger, stronger people across the creek as a kind of pulley so that those of

The Incarnational Marks of the Church

the group who were smaller would have an anchor for their crossing. Like a baptismal rising from the waters of death, we went through the waters to the other side. We knew we had one more crossing, but the creek ahead was shallower and thus safer. Adrenaline can motivate one's body and spirit for a long time, and we forged ahead, down the trail with only two flashlight beams and my exhausted spirit to keep us going. We sang a lot of camp songs that night! The last two miles, closest to our camp and warm beds, were of course the hardest. Like any trip, the last mile or hour seems interminable. Exhaustion had crept into our feet and brains. We wanted to be back at camp, out of the wind and rain, and in a warm sleeping bag. Finally, at 3.30 a.m. we dragged ourselves into the main lodge, made some warm drinks, and huddled together to celebrate our adventure and safe return. For the remainder of our days at camp, we grew together into a kind of spiritual wilderness family—no doubt bonded from our ridiculous adventure of twenty two miles in the dark of night. I knew we had come close to the edge of hypothermia, of losing someone down a raging mountain creek, of collapsing from exhaustion. It wasn't long after that summer that the camp sent out tents instead of tarps, and I never again trusted Minnesota youths who said that they had adequate rain gear. No doubt we had probably gone too far that night, but we had also gained something that would only come from life on the edge of a mountain pass. Somehow, hiking in the middle of the mountains, passing through icy creek waters, and finding our way home together, we felt the vulnerability and adventure that life brings. Life has a ragged edge, where passion and adventure come together. The time together was a sacrament of sorts, where we passed through the dangerous waters to the other side and became a family of a kind, and where everyone belonged, and where warm drinks shared together in the middle of the night became the nourishment that bound us together as a new kind of family. We had experienced a kind of grace—not tame, but wild and fierce. Sometimes one has to leave the safety of the homeland, where security becomes an excuse for apathy, and embark on the trail, head to the mountain pass, and know in one's bones the adventure of life. It's a wisdom that comes only from the edge.

If home is the place that provides safety from the adventure and passion of life, then we must leave immediately. John Muir, naturalist and activist, warns me that home becomes dangerous when it lures me away from the mountain passes in our lives. While I know that any place can lead one to the fierce passion and grace of God, I occasionally need a physical reminder, and that is why I always head back to Montana. It's my spiritual birthplace: my church. The wind, rain, earth, and fire are the elements of our birthplace and our relatives in God's family. While there were moments in Christian history when nature and grace were rent asunder, there are many other voices who testify that these powerful, earthy elements are as much the places where God acts in the world as are the hearts of human beings. Church is where God's grace meets us at the ragged edges of our lives.

Expanding the incarnation from *who* and *when* to *where* changes the way we understand what it means to be church. It's more than a building renovation. Developing the notion of *imago Dei* to include all creation means that humans are not the only members of church.[3] I believe that our views of church must be widened and expanded, because so many feel excluded from its mission and purpose. Church should be the place of God's grace for all, the place from which we are never excluded. So, where should we find church? We can always go to the familiar places: cathedrals, local parishes, synod assemblies, pilgrimages to find saints and ancient relics, and amid the rites and rituals of the church. But if we want to widen our view, reshape the boundaries of our map, and alter our itineraries, and accompany those who are forging into new territories, we will either find new places for church or at least see the familiar ones with new eyes. To get the best view of church we should start with the widest angle for our lens. Here is where I propose that we start: First, we begin in the cathedral of the cosmos, in the sacramental understanding that all things finite bear the infinite, that all things are in Christ, who is the firstborn of all creation.[4] Second, we will travel to Athens with St. Paul and into the midst of daily life, with all of its joys and sorrows; and then with Dietrich Bonhoeffer. In these places, we find God and church in our relationships with one another, especially among strangers and enemies, those whom we fear and ignore. In Paul's speech to the Athenians, he reminds us that God is in the connections with the strangers, with those we find foreign. For in God, "we live and move and have our being."[5] Third, we will discover church in places of hospitality, in the local acts and practices that make God's creation a place of grace for all. Finally, we are called not to be tourists out to see the sites but to be pilgrims on the Jesus Way.[6]

 3. Sittler, *Gravity & Grace*, 14.
 4. Col 1:15–20 (NRSV).
 5. Acts 17:27 (NRSV).
 6 Eugene Peterson also uses the contrasting images of tourist and pilgrim in Peterson, *A Long Obedience in the Same Direction*.

The Incarnational Marks of the Church

The Church Universal

We Begin in the Cathedral of the Cosmos, in the Sacramental Understanding That All Things Finite Bear the Infinite, and Are in Christ, Who Is the Firstborn of All Creation.

I won't take us on a long, detailed journey through the history of ecclesiological debates about the definition of *church* and what it means. Many of those debates became turf wars where boundaries of us and them were demarcated and those who didn't fit the current customs of orthodoxy were sent into exile or excommunicated. Of course we are no different today. As I write this, American nuns are on a road trip of their own in protest of the Vatican's condemnations of their work and beliefs. However, where I have always expected to find church (that is, as a place of grace) is often where it can seem most absent. And where I have least expected to discover church is often where it can seem most present. Many times I have been most welcomed by those who have been most excluded from the boundaries of the institutional church.

I've also heard plenty of sermons reminding me that I can't find God and church on a golf course or sitting at home by myself. For a Lutheran like me, church has always been defined as the congregation of the saints in which the gospel is rightly taught and the sacraments rightly administered.[1] For all Christians, church is defined by practices that happen with particular peoples in particular places. Luther was always nervous about naming church as an abstraction—it was always *these* people, in *this* place, receiving *these* specific gifts of grace. However, when certain practices or certain people are identified as the *only way* church can happen, then the sacraments become a means of exclusion instead of practices of inclusion where God's grace is experienced by all.

The very place that should have given me spiritual sustenance was the same place that pushed me to its borders: the church in my hometown. As a child I remember sitting in my home congregation of Hope Lutheran in Bozeman, Montana. Every Sunday our pastor would preach for at least twenty minutes, and I willingly admit that most of the time I heard little and saw a lot. We had an unusual sanctuary. I gather it was even controversial when it was first designed and built by Oswald

---

1. Evangelical Lutheran Synod of Missouri, *Augsburg Confession*, article 7, "On the Church."

Berg, a local architect. On the north side of the sanctuary, large glass windows framed only with simple wood lines covered the entire length of the building. Through the four seasons I could watch the Baptists go to church across the street, look at the trees change from green to yellow, and watch the snow pile up in the winter. As a child I learned more from looking through the windows into God's creation than from listening to the thundering, ponderous sermons coming from the pastor. Later, in college when the pastor in my congregation was becoming more adamant that women should not be ordained, and I was becoming more certain that seminary would lead to my chosen vocation, I decided, along with my parents, to attend the Newman Center at Montana State University. Once again I ended up in a sanctuary whose large windows faced south onto the Hyalite and Spanish Peaks. Luckily this time the compassionate words from the local priest matched the beauty of the mountains. I have often thought that every Christian needs at least two spiritual homes, where in at least one of them, they are always welcome. The other spiritual sanctuary for me, besides the local Newman Center, was of course, the church camp I returned to every summer.

This is what I learned about being a Christian and being a part of church from my years at camp: that the mountain peaks were my cathedral, the large boulders my pew, and the birds and animals were part of the congregation. I learned that what it meant to be part of the Christian church was much broader, deeper, and more exciting than what I had learned from worshiping in my home congregation. When we drove up the Boulder River road past the other camps, our camp director would wonder why they built chapels instead of using the outdoors as the sanctuary of God. If one could be out in one of the most beautiful settings in the world, why would one want to be indoors to worship? He wasn't saying that church could only happen in the mountains or outdoors; Christians need to worship in whatever place they are called to be. But that was the point: we were called to worship in this great, rugged wilderness of Montana. This area was our sanctuary and to not be a part of it, not to worship out in it, seemed almost a sacrilege. So, unless it was pouring rain, we worshiped outdoors. We would gather in the large alpine meadow where daisies, harebells, forget-me-nots, and American bistort root shot up among the large boulders. Hicks Peak and Baboon Mountain rose from the pine-tree-covered ridges. But it wasn't just the mountains and flowers that formed the church around me; it was a vision of the place through its people and purpose.

The Incarnational Marks of the Church

The vision of Christikon, written in 1975, introduced me to the adventure of faith: "Basically, according to the camp's permanent director, the aim of Christikon is to provide an experiment in Christian living, an opportunity for self-discovery through work and play . . . And to maintain an uncluttered day, the community is as unstructured and unscheduled as possible."[2] Wristwatches weren't permitted, and the bell called us to come running for dinner, worship, and study. We also played as hard as we worked. The rugged landscape lent itself to an adventuresome spirit. It seemed like the whole world was lit with the passion of God. This was an antidote to the apathy of much of the world. This wasn't just some mountaintop experience where life was some constant Rocky Mountain high; it was an adventure in living in, with, and under, a kind of sacramental experiment in the intimacy of topography and theology. Whether it was having time to quiet down at the end of the day by meditating on the Scripture cards we were handed (cleverly called bread cards) or singing hymns as we hiked, I learned that God's creation was my first spiritual sanctuary where doxology came easily for me.

The early Hebrew poets who wrote Genesis 1 got the theological worldview just right; the cosmos is the cathedral of God, and all voices praise God together. Other biblical writers throughout Scripture echo the same sentiment—that God is not confined to buildings or temples, but God's home is in all creation, from heaven to earth.[3] And the earthy stuff that God has made is the vehicle for God's action in the world. Christians throughout the centuries have celebrated this promise that God is present in the world in the rituals of sacraments. I love the words from Pierre Teilhard de Chardin, a Roman Catholic Jesuit priest and paleontologist. His sacramental views affirmed that the material, natural world is the focus of God's grace. In his "Hymn to the Universe," he writes: "Since once again, Lord—though this time not in the forests of the Aisne but in the steppes of Asia—I have neither bread, nor wine, nor altar, I will raise myself beyond these symbols, up to the pure majesty of the real itself; I, your priest, will make the whole earth my altar and on it will offer you all the labours and sufferings of the world."[4] The earth is the altar of our praise and prayer, where we join all the voices who groan in travail. In no other place in the Christian tradition of which I am a part do we confirm

---

2. Staunton and Keur, *Jerkline to Jeep*, 51.
3. Acts 7:48; 17:16–33; Ps 145:15; Jer 23:23–24.
4. Teilhard de Chardin, "Hymn of the Universe," 19.

The Geography of God's Incarnation

the value of the material world more than in the sacramental acts of Eucharist and baptism. Bread and wine, fire and water, merge with the Word of God to confirm that God's place is with us, in this world, at this time. This binding of God to us is a Trinitarian act of creation, redemption, and new creation.

On my first trip to England and later to Ireland, I got in touch with what I jokingly call my inner Celt. The early Irish roots of Christianity spread into England and shaped the creative elements of the natural world into daily sacramental practices. Every day was a Eucharistic and baptismal celebration: every day moved from darkness to light, from evening to morning, from birth to death. St. Patrick, of course, is one of Celtic Christianity's patrons of wisdom. While the music to which his words are often set is a bit doleful, I nevertheless love the words of St. Patrick's Breastplate: "I Bind unto Myself Today." The organist who serves the congregation of which I am a worshiping member today always cringes when I pick this hymn, but I still insist we should sing it frequently, even once a week, until we really get it. The words should remind us of the power and presence of God at work in each of us and in the whole of creation:

> I bind unto myself today
> The strong name of the Trinity,
> By invocation of the same
> The Three in One and One in Three.
>
> I bind this day to me forever
> By power of faith, Christ's incarnation;
> His baptism in Jordan river,
> His death on Cross for my salvation;
> His bursting from the spicèd tomb,
> His riding up the heavenly way,
> His coming at the day of doom
> I bind unto myself today.
>
> I bind unto myself today
> The virtues of the starlit heaven,
> The glorious sun's life giving ray,
> The whiteness of the moon at even,
> The flashing of the lightning free,
> The whirling wind's tempestuous shocks,

The Incarnational Marks of the Church

The stable earth, the deep salt sea
Around the old eternal rocks.[5]

The early Celtic church celebrated the goodness of creation and the wildness of God's grace. Humans understood their vocation in relationship to all creation.[6] This isn't some sentimental worship of nature but a realization that all creation has a voice in the cathedral of God!

Experiences of mystery and transcendence in the outdoors center or recenter our usual view of our place in the world. We realize how much a part of the rest of the natural world we are, and that we are not always the center of it. This can be simultaneously a relief (that we are not the center of the universe) and frightening (that we are a smaller part of it than we have wanted to admit). While God placed humankind in the garden of Eden, we must remember that the garden is not a pristine paradise but a messy entanglement of weeds, growth, people, production, economics. And we must always remember that the world we live in is not just pretty places, not just the wilderness to which we like to retreat, God's world must include all that we have described as nature, as technonature. Place includes the cultural elements. Technonature is where God is, in the connections between the places and people.

The natural world is ambiguous and not always a safe place for everyone. I know that animals eat each other, that rivers overflow their banks and destroy the wildlife and human homes. I have seen fire burn away the green of trees and grass. Sometimes we mask our prayers with pious words that reflect our fear of the ragged edges of life, where life and death meet the grace of God. Just once I hope that those of us who mark ourselves as church can be honest enough with God to express just how strangely ambiguous this world really is: good, not perfect—this creation of ours. Church must be the place where we can express in our prayers and hymns the fears and hopes we have about this God who has placed us in this cathedral of creation, where of all voices can give praise to God for life and love, and where we can celebrate the mass of all creation so that everything is blessed and met with God's fiery and passionate love.

---

5. Evangelical Lutheran Church in America, *Evangelical Lutheran Worship*, Hymn #450.

6. De Waal, *Every Earthly Blessing*, 56.

The Geography of God's Incarnation

The Church Apostolic

We Travel to Athens with the Apostle Paul to Encounter Those Who Are Foreign and Other. And Also We Go with the Apostle Bonhoeffer into the Midst of Our Daily Lives, with All of Our Joys and Sorrows. In These Places, We Find God and Church in Our Relationships with One Another, Especially among the Strangers and Enemies, Those Whom We Fear and Ignore.

> While Paul was waiting for them in Athens, he was deeply distressed to see that the city was full of idols. So he argued in the synagogue with the Jews and the devout persons, and also in the market-place every day with those who happened to be there. Also some Epicurean and Stoic philosophers debated with him. Some said, "What does this babbler want to say?" Others said, "He seems to be a proclaimer of foreign divinities." (This was because he was telling the good news about Jesus and the resurrection.) So they took him and brought him to the Areopagus and asked him, "May we know what this new teaching is that you are presenting? It sounds rather strange to us, so we would like to know what it means." Now all the Athenians and the foreigners living there would spend time in nothing but telling or hearing something new.
>
> Then Paul stood in front of the Areopagus and said, "Athenians, I see how extremely religious you are in every way. For as I went through the city and looked carefully at the objects of your worship, I found among them an altar with the inscription, 'To an unknown god.' What therefore you worship as unknown, this I proclaim to you. The God who made the world and everything in it, he who is Lord of heaven and earth, does not live in shrines made by human hands, nor is he served by human hands, as though he needed anything, since he himself gives to all mortals life and breath and all things. From one ancestor he made all nations to inhabit the whole earth, and he allotted the times of their existence and the boundaries of the places where they would live, so that they would search for God and perhaps grope for him and find him—though indeed he is not far from each one of us. For 'In him we live and move and have our being'; as even some of your own poets have said, 'For we too are his offspring.' Since we are God's offspring, we ought not to think the deity is like gold or silver or stone, an image formed by the art and imagination of mortals. While God has overlooked the times

The Incarnational Marks of the Church

of human ignorance, now he commands all people everywhere to repent, because he has fixed a day on which he will have the world judged in righteousness by a man whom he has appointed, and of this he has given assurance to all by raising him from the dead."

When they heard of the resurrection of the dead, some scoffed; but others said, "We will hear you again about this." At that point Paul left them.[7]

It takes nine chapters in the book of Acts to get to the conversion of Saul. We know that he persecuted those who "belonged to the Way." Ironically, of course, while Saul was on the way (to Damascus), he encounters Jesus. For three days he loses his sight and must be led around by others. A disciple called Ananias receives a vision from Jesus that he must find Saul and heal him from his blindness. By chapter 13 of Acts, Luke uses the Roman form of Saul's name: Saul becomes Paul as he sets out on his missionary trips, primarily to the lands of Gentiles. While I was first reading the book of Acts, I read the section just quoted from chapter 17 as a text about respectful evangelism. Prior to this chapter, in Acts 13, Paul first preaches in Antioch, in the synagogue to the Jews: he utilizes the stories of the Jewish faith; he is speaking to insiders. He moves from the stories of the land of Egypt to the stories of King David, only to wind up at the River Jordan where Jesus is baptized. All roads lead finally to Jesus, the Way. However, in the seventeenth chapter of Acts, Paul arrives in Athens again. This time he preaches not only in the synagogues but also in the marketplace. And he preaches a different sermon in this different location. He leaves out the details of Israel's past, and instead draws on the philosophy and poetry of the Greeks, who were Gentiles. Instead of merely crossing the boundary into their world, Paul establishes a common boundary between both worlds that the creation in which they live and move and have their being is made by God. This God has created everyone and establishes a place for everyone. Furthermore, this God is not a God out there but is the God who is nearby. And this nearby God is the one who announces repentance, judgment, and salvation for all. Because God resurrected Jesus from the dead, salvation is for all. They have a common Creator and a common Savior, God, incarnate in Jesus the Christ. All ways are open through the Jesus Way.

While this text could surely be read with sympathetic lenses to postmodern concerns about diversity, I wonder if I have missed

---

7. Acts 17:16–33 (NRSV).

something in the text. So, I read it again with the help of others. For example, David Tiede, a Lutheran biblical scholar, reminds me that the exchanges between Paul and the philosophers have an "edge." They exchange insults about each other's interpretation of God. "When the philosophers call Paul a 'babbler,' their insult is an elegant wordplay in Greek. The Stoics were focused on the 'seminal reason of the universe,' the *spermatikos logos*. They regard Paul as a *spermologos*, a seed picker, searching for words. In turn, Paul was on the firing line with the philosophers, calling them unknowing in their worship, even ignorant."[8] Paul doesn't satisfy either the Epicureans or the Stoics with his evaluation of their gods or their analysis of the human condition. But he did pique their interest. Tiede claims that Paul was able to get beyond the insults and hear in all their claims a common longing for that which is spiritual, for something more. This is a human spiritual yearning, and Paul understands and proclaims that this human yearning is satisfied by a God who became human.[9] God understands us because God became human. However, if this didn't sound strange enough for an audience that likely had a hope for immortality of the soul, Paul's announcement that human bodies were resurrected would have been gross to their sensibilities. We are not so different than the Athenians; most of us are pious docetists or gnostics who can't imagine that our flesh is worthy of redemption. This sermon of Paul helps us to see that the gospel of God in Jesus Christ is for us in this world, not for some other people in another heavenly world. Right here. Right now. We have the same universal spiritual longing as the Athenians, and it is answered in the particular person of Jesus Christ.[10] This God meets us where people are, and meets them in their particular body-selves.

Where in the world is God? When we ask this question we discover where church is. We should pay attention like St. Paul does to the location of those around us, and to our own place in the world. And we can learn from, respect, and honor the places of others while remaining grounded in our own traditions and narratives. But that isn't enough, at least, according to the author of Acts. We must, amid our diversity and difference, find common ground in the creation. For here we know each other as created co-creators, made by God for each other to be at work

---

8. Tiede, "The God Who Made the World," 55.
9. Ibid., 57.
10. Skinner, "Commentary on Acts 17:22–31."

in the world. And this work in the world is our vocation, taking care of each other, so that we have a common ground that isn't shattered by divisions, war, and devastation. Does the church foster common ground or create such divisions that the unity of God's creation is broken and destroyed? What difference does it make that the church is on the Jesus Way instead of another way? We cannot use our plurality to avoid our common ground, but neither can we use our common ground as a place from which we condemn and do violence to one another. While I hope this is true among Christians, how much more do I hope that we, when establishing common ground as creatures, can lean forward with anticipation as we learn from and with those from other religious traditions.

What happens when Christians preach to different communities? Who is the audience, and what is their location? The rather simplistic and yet profound answer is, of course: where you are at that moment in time. In a recent assessment of the mission of the Lutheran church in North America, David Tiede used this text from Acts 17 to talk discuss our current social and cultural location. He writes: "When we 'interpret the present time' by observing Lutheran social realities in North America, we see a community with a largely northern European history, now shifting from rural to urban, with a diminishing and aging membership. With the secular pundits we observe Christendom's decline. In rising world Christianity, we also hear the dislocated cultures protesting globalization."[11] To understand the mission of the church means that Christians should read and study not only texts included in the Christian Scriptures but also texts and traditions of those from other places. Text and context become inextricably linked in the navigation of the Christian way in the world. Concerning evangelism, Tiede claims that it is "not about guarding Lutheran boundaries of doctrinal purity but about going public from the center: Christ crucified and raised."[12] He might as well have quoted Dietrich Bonhoeffer, a fellow Lutheran interpreter of text and context. Church happens in the center of the village, not at the edges where we can exclude ourselves and God from the troubles of the world.

What difference does it make to the world that the Christian church is in it? Dietrich Bonhoeffer found that the church of his time had failed; it only served people on the margins of their lives and was not relevant at the center. A centerless church provided, of course, a perfect setup for

---

11. Tiede, "The God Who Made the World," 52.
12. Ibid.

The Geography of God's Incarnation

the German churches to follow Hitler. This young German theologian raised sharp and haunting questions about who and what church was. He believed that where we often expect to find church it is most absent, and where we least expect to find church is where it is most present. Bonhoeffer grew up in a family that rarely attended church, and throughout his own career he was known for his sharp attacks on the church. Like St. Paul, Bonhoeffer didn't locate church in a building or institution but in the incarnate One: God in Christ, the theological center of the faith.

In one of his last letters from Tegel prison, Bonhoeffer writes to his friend Eberhard Bethge about his most troubling theological questions. Bonhoeffer even warns Bethge that he might be troubled by what he was thinking and writing. At a time when he faced his own ragged edge of life, the questions of his faith were most poignant and piercing. To put it simply, Bonhoeffer asks: What is Christianity? Who is Christ? But he doesn't ask those questions as abstract theological questions that will require abstract theological speculation. He asks them with the notion that they matter for now. Now, in this situation, for these people and time, what is Christianity, and who is Christ? Bonhoeffer responds that if Christianity is religion as he knows and defines it, then Christianity has failed. Bonhoeffer looks at the German church and other churches in the modern West and indicts them for their peddling of "cheap grace." Sounding much like Martin Luther, his Reformation counterpart almost five hundred years earlier, Bonhoeffer criticizes religion as the pious trappings that have covered the Christian church for almost two thousand years: all the rituals, words, beliefs, and doctrines that keep people from actually living as Christians shaped by the gospel of Jesus Christ. Bonhoeffer even says that Christianity must shed its religion, that the world has come of age, and that religion has failed. He writes: "The time when people could be told everything by means of words, whether theological or pious, is over, and so is the time of inwardness and conscience—and that means the time of religion in general. We are moving towards a completely religionless time; people as they are now simply cannot be religious any more. Even those who honestly describe themselves as 'religious' do not in the last act up to it, and so they presumably mean something quite different by 'religious.'"[13] In a time that he determines as an "emergency," Bonhoeffer rejects religion and calls for a religionless Christianity. What does he mean by that?

---

13. Kelly and Nelson, eds., *A Testament to Freedom*, 501.

Bonhoeffer worries that religion has pushed God out to the boundaries to the places where we find God only when God is needed and humans have failed. Whether we pray to God for a parking place or run to God at the last moment when all else fails, God seems superfluous to the world around us. God is out there somewhere, summoned into our lives when we need last minute intervention. And God also was out there in the bourgeois German culture, summoned only for the ritual baptisms, confirmations, marriages, and burials. It sounds familiar, even now. Conveniently left aside, God and religion became redundant. A student of mine put it so well: "If we spend our entire time running up to heaven to find God, when God all along has been here on earth amidst us, we will pass each other by."[14] We expect to find God in heaven waiting to be asked into our world, when God has been in our midst all along, waiting for us to help! Or to use Bonhoeffer's words: "God is beyond in the midst of our life. The church stands, not at the boundaries where human powers give out, but in the middle of the village."[15]

And the notion that Christ is no longer an object of religion or piety, but Christ is the Lord of all creation seems suddenly radical. Christ becomes the subject not the object of faith. God is not just found along the outer boundaries of our life, but God is at the center of creation, the God of life and goodness. "It always seems to me that we are trying anxiously in this way to reserve some space for God; I should like to speak of God not on the boundaries but at the center, not in weaknesses but in strength; and therefore not in death and guilt but in man's life and goodness."[16] Bonhoeffer confirms that God is at the center. This is an affirmation of the goodness of life, of being a creature of God. Tiede interprets St. Paul's sermon to the Athenians in the same manner: "Paul's speech in Athens is a public confession, a scriptural foundation for every generation's faith and practice of evangelism. Paul in Athens also interprets the world as God's creation, destined by Jesus' resurrection to be restored as the arena of God's justice and mercy."[17] When God is at the center, we can face all the ragged edges of our life with hope and grace and mercy. Even when life seemed most dangerous and full of despair, Bonhoeffer remembered

---

14. Thank you, Shane LeClaire!
15. Kelly and Nelson, eds., *A Testament to Freedom*, 503.
16. Ibid.
17. Tiede, "The God Who Made the World," 54.

to thank God for the thrush who sang in the prison courtyard each morning outside his window.

St. Paul, Dietrich Bonhoeffer, and David Tiede remind me that the quotidian is the place of God's grace.[18] Tiede connects place with community, text with context in this meeting of God's grace with our world: "Our awe for the mundane also means holy regard for all we meet. In a consumer society, we treat people as customers, not all bad if you're buying. But how will we deal with others, family members and strangers, in the faith that God was at work in their lives before we showed up? With what eyes will we see the man mowing the hotel lawn or the mother with her children in the market or the scientist in the laboratory?"[19] Where does the church need to be? Is the church in a building? I'm not sure what church will be if we only think of it as a place to worship, as the place where sacred reality is. I would love to think that awe for the mundane means that we have holy regard for all we meet. I wonder if the church, as it is, is working? That's a question that people both within and without the church's boundaries are asking. One place where I know the questions are being responded to occurs in the dialogue between traditional congregations and the new, emergent churches.

In a blog post for *Patheos* Phyllis Tickle offers her thoughts on "the theology of place as it informs both the inherited church and fresh expressions of church."[20] She then relates her experience of visiting a congregation of senior citizens led by a younger pastor informed by the emergent church traditions. No surprise comes to readers that Tickle reaches the conclusion that the itinerant nature of the emergent church needs the anchor of the institutional church. I might agree. What I long to see even more in these discussions is the realization that a theology of place is about not only where we are, but also where God is. I will listen to and read more of these emerging voices. Interesting enough is that they have drawn on the mothers and fathers of the early church, whose practices of hospitality shape the message of God's grace for all.

---

18. I am also grateful for the interpretive and homiletical work of Michael Rogness. Rogness, "Proclaiming the Gospel on Mars Hill," 274–94.
19. Tiede, "The God Who Made the World," 61.
20. Tickle, "An Assessment of Great Worth."

The Church Sacramental

We Discover Church in Places of Hospitality, in the Local Acts and Practices That Make God's Creation a Place of Grace for All.

In a somewhat uncharacteristic move for this book, I want to take a theological detour of sorts to the historical discussions about the sacramental practices during the Reformation. For here, buried in the heated rhetoric of the Reformation, we might unearth language that can help us relocate the understanding of church as the practices of those people who are in particular places in particular times. Luther argued with the other Reformers, particularly with Ulrich Zwingli, about the location of God in the world, about what the real presence of God means to the world, and consequently what this meant for being church. These arguments reflect the tensions of the day; the church had fractured into a million pieces, and people were afraid that the center wouldn't hold. But each fractured group sought to find the center in a different place. Luther feared most of all that Christ was being pushed out of the center of people's lives and into other places: the structures of the institution, the literal reading of Scripture, the trust in rituals and rites, and into the realms of the heavens and the world hereafter. And in none of these places did Luther see the real presence of Christ, active and powerful in the lives of people and in creation. Where is God in the world? And where is the church?

According to Martin Luther: in Jesus the Christ, whose presence is real and right here, right now, that is where the church is. According to Luther, church is where the gospel is preached and the sacraments are administered. But about not just any church did Luther speak. Luther spoke about particularity: this church and these people. He spoke of particular means: exacting, fastidious, precise, noteworthy, unique, specific, distinct, details. The definition of church is not abstract. Like the words we quoted as a child when we formed our hands into a church: "Here's the church; here's the steeple. Open the door and see all the people." Not in heaven up above but right here amid the people we find the church. And not just among any people but among these people, in this church, blessed by God's grace for this day. Richard Rohr, a Franciscan theologian, writes, "In Franciscan thinking, this specific, individual, concrete thing is always God's work and God's continuing choice, precisely in its uniqueness, not in its uniformity. Duns Scotus called it 'thisness.'"[21] Like

---

21. Rohr, *Falling Upward*, 56.

Scotus, Martin Luther paid attention to the details, to what "mattered." In his treatises about the sacraments, Luther wrote about God present in "this meal" at "this table." God's grace was always *pro nobis*: for you (plural) but also for you (singular).

Church means that we must practice what we preach and pray. History reminds us that some of the arguments about church were over its rituals and practices, for they highlighted questions about God's action in the world and in believers' lives. For example, Luther's arguments over the practice of the sacraments are some of the fiercest in Reformation theologies. Andreas Karlstadt spiritualized the sacraments in a move away from Luther and Rome, and Zwingli followed. Zwingli and Anabaptists tried to purge the theologies and sacramental practices of Rome from their worship. This was understandable, but Luther felt that these had gone too far and had removed the presence of Christ from the real world. In many ways, Luther's understanding of the real presence was more at home within a Catholic sacramental framework. The two treatises "That These Words of Christ, 'This Is My Body,' etc., Still Stand Firm against the Fanatics, 1527" and "Confession Concerning Christ's Supper, 1528" along with "Against the Heavenly Prophets," stand as Luther's strongest works on the sacraments and Christology.[22] Martin Luther's arguments with the Sacramentarians proceed with a discussion about where God is present in the Eucharist. These historic discussions can give us insight into how we interpret God's place in the world. While the polemical language might seem too heated for our times, Luther thought the very nature of the gospel was at stake and so we can simultaneously understand his passion, and yet hope not to repeat his transgressions and condemnation of those with whom he disagreed.

The doctrine of the incarnation is at the heart and center of the controversies. Luther argues with Zwingli about *where* God is present. The arguments over scripture are rooted in Christological disagreements. Luther accuses Zwingli of spiritualizing the Eucharist and diminishing the humanity of God. Luther rants: "It is precisely the same devil who now assails us through the fanatics by blaspheming the holy and venerable sacrament of our Lord Jesus Christ, out of which they would like to make mere bread and wine as a symbol or memorial sign of Christians, in whatever their dream or fancy dictates. They will not grant that the Lord's body and blood are present, even though the plain, clear words stand

---

22. Fischer, et al., "Introduction to Volume 37," in *Luther's Works 37: Word and Sacrament*, III, herein cited as LW.

right there: 'Eat, this is my body.' Yet those words still stand firm and invulnerable against them."²³ While the argument is not quite the same, Kathleen Norris accuses Americans of spiritualizing the land. For her, the Dakotas are not an abstraction; they are the physical place of God's sacramental presence. And so, church, is not an abstraction; it is people, in God's presence, in a particular place and time.

When Luther addresses the "distance" between God and the world, he speaks from experience and not abstract doctrinal formulations. The doctrine of creation is the "place" from which to understand the sacraments. Luther: "And it is grounded actually in the first article, where I say, 'I believe in God the Father almighty, maker of heaven and earth.' Precisely this article shields and sustains our interpretation of the Supper, as we have heard."²⁴ He also claims that God's presence is manifest in God's goodness and power: "The Scriptures teach us, however, that the right hand of God is not a specific place in which a body must or may be, such as on a golden throne, but is the almighty power of God, which at one and the same time can be nowhere and yet must be everywhere."²⁵ Place is the power of God's presence in, with, and under!

Luther wrote that limiting God to only one place is dangerous. God is both here and now, and yet everywhere in general. Luther writes: "The first is this article of our faith, that Jesus Christ is essential, natural, true, complete God and man in one person, undivided and inseparable. The second, that the right hand of God is everywhere. The third, that the Word of God is not false or deceitful. The fourth, that God has and knows various ways to be present at a certain place, not only the single one of which the fanatics prattle, which the philosophers call the 'local.'"²⁶ How and where is God present? Luther asks Zwingli, "How can it be true at one and the same time that God is entirely present, personally and essentially, in Christ on earth as in his mother's womb, in the crib, in the temple, in the wilderness, in cities, in the garden, in the field, on the cross, in the grave, etc., yet nonetheless in the Father's bosom?"²⁷ Luther answers with this: "Rather, it is one person with God, so that wherever God is, there also is the man; God also is said

---

23. LW 37:18.
24. LW 37:69.
25. LW 37:57.
26. LW 37:214.
27. LW, 37:61.

The Geography of God's Incarnation

to suffer."[28] Wherever we see the suffering of others, hidden here and there, where we least expect to find God, God has promised to be present for us. God's presence is hidden in the opposites . . . not in the places of glory, but in the moments of the cross.

Our bodies are the places in which God works and is present. This real presence of God is not found in celestial realms but here in our body, our whole body. Luther writes: "it is a glory and praise of his inexpressible grace and mercy that he concerns himself so profoundly with us poor sinners and shows us such gracious love and goodness, not content to be everywhere in and around, above and beside us, but even giving us his own body as nourishment, in order that with such a pledge, he may assure and promise us that our body too shall live forever, because it partakes on earth of an everlasting and living food."[29] And so the physical acts of drinking and eating are the places in which we receive God. Where is God? Where are we? For sure, we know in the practices of grace, in the sacraments. Luther says, "the sacrament is not the sign of the absent body of Christ but is the body of Christ himself, as that by which is our body physically fed but also the nature and substance of our body is nourished, strengthened, and sustained unto eternal life and becomes a member of the body of Christ."[30] When we eat and drink together, we share in God's presence. What makes the meal a place of grace is God's promise of faithfulness. God binds God's self to the physical, embodied acts of our lives.

The acts of eating and drinking in the Lord's Supper are not only for faithful ones but must be offered to all of God's creation. As the words of Teilhard suggest, God's mass is for all. Luther notes, "On this we take our stand, and we also believe and teach that in the Supper we eat and take to ourselves Christ's body truly and physically. But how this takes place or how he is in the bread, we do not know and are not meant to know. God's Word we should believe without setting bounds or measure to it. The bread we see with our eyes, but we hear with our ears that Christ's body is present."[31] The finite truly bears the infinite presence of God. Luther gets to the heart of questions about God's presence in the world.[32] When Christ is present, he binds us to a particular place. We can go about grop-

---

28. LW, 37:222.
29. LW, 37:71.
30. LW, 37:119.
31. LW, 37:29.
32. LW, 37:219, in "Confession Concerning Christ's Supper," where he is addressing the two natures.

ing for God's presence generally everywhere, in no place in particular. But when Christ is present it is in particularity. Of course, we must accept that this particularity is just that: particular and not abstract. The controversies about what we eat, and when we eat, are part of the particularity. Christians have argued about the sacraments for centuries and continue to do so even now. We have even condemned and excommunicated one another. The real presence of Christ is manifest even when our particularity gets the best of us! I realize that beneath all our divisions and particularities is the promise of unity brought about by God's gracious love.

I find that contemporary discussions of the Eucharist by Roman Catholics sound much like the words of Martin Luther:

We become catholic together in our sharing of these Eucharistic moments, when we celebrate the truly universal sharing of God's grace for all. When we break bread together, in all meals of grace and mercy, we become church. It's not just in a specific celebration of the meal in a ceremony on a Sunday morning that we find God, but in all our meals shared together as companions in God's creation. This is church. And I have seen it happen where I have been taught to least expect it.

I love the following words from Kathleen Norris. While she is not explaining a sacramental way of knowing and living as such, I think she gets it just right about our knowing that it happens deep within a place. She writes:

> Conversion means starting with who we are, not who we wish we were. It means knowing where we come from . . . It was in moving back to the Plains that I found my old ones, my flesh and blood ancestors as well as the desert monks and mystics of the Christian church. Dakota is where it all comes together, and surely that is one definition of the sacred.[33]

People are the heart of place. One of our friends with whom we gather is a poet who knows his place in the world. Another friend is an artist whose art is literally grounded in this same kind of knowing. Sheila paints the locations where the poet Jerome lives. People are the heart of place. The Freemans know this and have taught this to me.

They used to have a great liturgical event on the prairie every fall when they celebrated St. Crispin's Day (the patron saint of shoes). Everyone would await the invitation that arrived in the mail announcing the annual feast of renewing friendships, hiking along the mowed prairie

---

33. Norris, *Dakota*, 131.

paths, and listening to the bagpipe player serenading the crowds. Mary Freeman served up a cauldron of chili, the aroma of warm spices mixed with the stacks of apple pies and other desserts on ladders nearby. The Freemans created hospitality, like the nuns and monks who were their spiritual mentors. The Benedictines, akin to the Freemans, practice the art of extravagant hospitality—in the place they inhabit. To walk along the Freeman property with Mary as your guide is to know what it means to experience grace. She knows the prairie flowers and trees by name and has tended carefully to every acre of their land. The Freemans practice church. All are welcome. I think of all those bodies that the church has not wanted to let enter in its sanctuaries at some point. In many institutional religious settings, people are excluded from becoming pastors, from leading worship, and from feeling welcome simply because of their sex, race, age, economic class, ability level, or sexual orientation.

Creating a hospitable sanctuary must start from the very beginning so that all who enter are able to find their place, to make it their spiritual home. That's hard work, and it takes practice. Compassion and hospitality are not concepts but embodied actions. Compassion and hospitality might be the most important means by which we practice being who God intended us to be as the body of Christ. One must travel to the Freemans' place, walk the mowed paths, eat a bowl of chili, and be greeted by Mary and Jerome. They are, like Sheila: artists and poets who reveal hospitality to those of us who long to be touched by such embodied grace. No one knows better than the Freemans what it means to interpret this passage from Ecclesiastes 2:24: "There is nothing better for mortals than to eat and drink, and find enjoyment in their toil." We always leave their home as different people, transformed.

For over thirty years I have had one foot in the Lutheran church and the other within Roman Catholicism, particularly with the Benedictines. I believe that the first time I felt really accepted into a Roman Catholic parish was when my husband taught at Catholic schools in Chicago, and I helped out occasionally, teaching flute and piano students. Every summer the faculty and staff worked at the school carnival to raise monies for various school programs. Even as a part-time faculty member, I knew I couldn't say no to the principal, an equally demanding and gracious Franciscan nun. We were assigned to work in the Bingo area, and the memory I carry with me of that night is the smoke that gathered in clouds under the outdoor tents, and that the mother of one of my flute

The Incarnational Marks of the Church

students, who desperately needed a new instrument, won the jackpot that night. The next week the student had a shiny, new sterling silver flute.

As the months went by at this school, we even received the sacrament. (I don't think the priest could turn us down since we attended mass more than many of his real parishioners). Two of the fifth-grade teachers invited me to come to talk with their classes about women in ministry; I even wore my clerical collar. One little boy who had my husband for elementary band was totally flummoxed and asked, "Where do you sleep? With the nuns or with your husband?" In a way, I had completely displaced his notions of where I belonged. But in his funny and utmost quizzical manner, I knew that something had happened to both of us in this exchange. But finally it was receiving a dinner invitation to the sisters' home for an evening meal that brought my husband and me into the full inclusion of the life at this parish. We left this suburban parish, after six amazing years. We loved the strong sacramental life, the fellowship with the Catholic sisters, and the joys of being surrounded by schoolchildren who could integrate faith and learning every day.

My husband, Gary, not only taught elementary and middle-school instrumental music, but also had a rather large chorus of second- through sixth-graders. Since I had been invited to the fifth-grade class to talk about becoming a Lutheran pastor, Gary and I decided to reciprocate and invite his hundred-voice children's choir to the Lutheran seminary for worship. On a spring day in Hyde Park a yellow school bus opened its doors, and about one hundred children in plaid jumpers and blue pants walked into the Lutheran seminary. I don't know who was more surprised that day—the seminarians, who had never seen such a young group help to lead worship in such a professional way; or the Catholic schoolchildren, who were somewhat horrified at the sloppy liturgical manners of the seminarians. However, for one brief day, the boundaries between denominations that once gave rise to mutual condemnation and violence were crossed, and a kind of ecumenical resurrection took place. The old and tired ways of being Lutheran and Roman Catholic opened up through children's voices and seminarians' gratitude for their presence.

Weekly Eucharist in the Chicago Catholic parish became such a habit for us that we couldn't imagine worship without it. So, when we moved to Sioux Falls, South Dakota, we decided to find a Lutheran church where we could have weekly Eucharist. We couldn't find any place, and for months we tried one church after another. Finally, when a colleague of mind at work said they needed some help with music at his parish, we decided to try it. From the moment we entered St. Michael's Roman Catholic Parish, we felt welcome. We eventually heard about the parish as *the* place in Sioux Falls to worship, where new ways of being church were happening. We experienced the sanctuary's gathering place, and understood the importance of the gardens planted for a food pantry. We received the invitation not only to be on the worship committee and help with worship, but also to give our monies and time. For a brief time, we were even put on the membership roster and received the *Bishop's Bulletin*. Still trying to find a place within our Lutheran tradition, we eventually joined a congregation, and we are still members there. But that was a time in which Lutherans still didn't have weekly Eucharist in these parts of the Dakotas. When parishes first popped up on the vast Dakota plains, they came with their pietistic Norwegian roots, and their anti-institutional/anti-Catholic sentiments. Weekly communion sounded too Roman, and we also heard that surely it would lose its special character if it was received too often. Once again, I longed for that weekly meal where I knew that God's grace was available to be shared among a community I knew as church. So we stayed members in two churches, feeling more at home in the Roman Catholic congregation and less at home in our own Lutheran tradition.

I have discovered along the way that I am not the only person who holds within me multiple religious identities. I have learned that denominations are really abstractions, groups with an identity, but with no specific face or place. When I worshiped in Chicago or in Sioux Falls, the place was the people, the community embodied in practices. The ecumenical culture during those years was gracious. Lutherans, Roman Catholics, and Baptists worked together to create the Banquet, a place for those who needed to eat but couldn't afford to do so. They could find a meal and companionship. When I went through an unexpected, but life-threatening surgery, the two priests from St. Michael's came to visit me. In one fleeting moment, when I realized how close I had come to possibly dying during a surgery, I even asked the two Catholic priests when I died, if they would preside at my funeral. To this day, I would still be grateful if they honor that request. Nonetheless, as the old adage goes, times change, and with the changes came different leadership in the climate of ecumenism, on both local and global levels. We began to realize, with a lot of accompanying grief, that our time at St. Michael's needed to come to an end. For for the years in which we felt included by the priests and parishioners, we have been thankful.

The Incarnational Marks of the Church

We are all strangers in a way and need to find refuge and sanctuary in another's tradition. The Benedictines practice hospitality, welcoming the stranger. "Listen" is the first word of the Rule of St. Benedict. I've been a guest multiple times at St. John's Abbey in Collegeville, Minnesota, and at St. Benedict's nearby. They have welcomed me not just as a guest at the guesthouse but as a scholar, friend, and companion along the way. Both communities are known as refuges for those of us who might occasionally feel like strangers in our own churches. These monasteries have often been on the border themselves, and Lutheranism started from a monastic community. I forget about that. For all the talk that Luther repudiated his monastic background, he also cherished much of it—in particular the values of hospitality, community, and taking in the neighbor. Monastic communities have been on borders, at the edges of wilderness. Lindisfarne is a great example of the way that Christianity entered England. Many of us still go to those border places because it is on the border that we might feel most welcome. When we experience displacement from our own church, we might feel threatened to cross fully into the land of another one. But we can rest at the borders, in the sanctuaries of another who welcome our crossing from one threshold into another.

The Church Eschatological

We Are Called not to Be Tourists out to See the Sites, but to Be Pilgrims on the Jesus Way.

Home, Away, and Home Again: Sharing the Conditions

We are called not to be tourists out to see the sites, but to be pilgrims on the Jesus Way.

"The Word became flesh and made his home among us."[34]
There are different ways to travel. Sometimes I simply want to be a tourist, to go and see the sites. I love being a tourist; it is in my blood. Every summer my parents and I took a trip. We traveled by train, on the old Northern Pacific, to Chicago and on to Pennsylvania. One year we even got a sleeper car, and we looked out from the vista dome and ate our meals in the dining car. Other years we drove together to the mountains or to the ocean. I loved those family vacations and have made a point to

34. John 1:14 (CEB).

always do the same in my adult life. Gary and I love to travel, love to be tourists. Sometimes the preparation for the trip is as much fun as the trip itself. My husband and I love to look at maps, imagining which roads we will take and where we will stop. For days we plan what gear to take, and how it will all fit into our suitcase. No matter how long we are gone, it never seems long enough. We always wish we could have seen more, learned more, and stayed longer in one place. That's the problem, I suppose, with being a tourist. You never really get to know the sites or the people you meet along the way. And really, the point of being a tourist is to see the sites.

Americans have become particularly adept at being tourists. My worst experiences of being a tourist seem to always occur on busses with lots of other people, being hauled from one place to another. One summer we were chaperones, along with several other adults, for over two hundred high school students on a band and choir trip to Europe. We were bussed everywhere; most of the kids slept. By the end, we had been to five countries in sixteen days. I don't remember much of the tour. Like the students, I slept through the sites, suffering from long lectures about this and that. This trip brings to mind the famous quote I have used so many times from Annie Dillard about what it means to be a part of the church. She accuses Christians of being brainless tourists on a guided tour of the absolute! Christianity is not a guided tour, but an active engagement with the world. I quote her again, for she gets it just right, her critique of Christians:

> On the whole, I do not find Christians, outside of the catacombs, sufficiently sensible of conditions. Does anyone have the foggiest idea what sort of power we so blithely invoke? Or, as I suspect, does no one believe a word of it? The churches are children playing on the floor with their chemistry sets, mixing up a batch of TNT to kill a Sunday morning. It is madness to wear ladies' straw hats and velvet hats to church; we should all be wearing crash helmets. Ushers should issue life preservers and signal flares; they should lash us to our pews. For the sleeping god may wake someday and take offense, or the waking god may draw us out to where we can never return.[35]

Annie Dillard's prophetic voice calls us out of passivity and into action. There are ways to simply see the sights, and then there are ways to engage the world, to walk with others along the ragged edge of life. God

35. Dillard, *Teaching a Stone to Talk*, 51–52.

doesn't call the church to be brainless tourists on packaged tour of the absolute. God calls us to be pilgrims on the Jesus Way.

More than any other prayer in the Christian tradition, I love this one from Vespers. For me, it summarizes the vocation of the Christian church: "O God, you have called your servants to ventures of which we cannot see the ending, by paths as yet untrodden, through perils unknown. Give us faith to go out with good courage, not knowing where we go, but only that your hand is leading us and your love supporting us; through Jesus Christ our Lord. Amen."[36] To go on a pilgrimage is to embark on a quest with meaning and purpose. And we can't go alone. We must join with all the saints along the Jesus Way. Just as some of us took the backpacking journey into the wilderness of Montana that I earlier described in the chapter, we are called, I believe, to go to the ragged edges of life, to the borders between life and death, to bear witness to and accompany other travelers through their sufferings in life. An early church father and historian called this "sharing the conditions."[37] When we share the conditions of our fellow travelers, we will enter into the moments of their lives, their pain and suffering, their joys and delights. We will share bread together along the way. Pilgrimage is a Eucharistic journey.

This pilgrim journey of the Christian faith is like a journey through the movements of the human life-cycle: home, away, and home again. We all begin somewhere and initially call it home, and at some point in our lives, whether literally or metaphorically, we leave and return again. This threefold movement came to life for me when I heard a lecture by Jeremy Begbie, an Anglican theologian and musician, who compared the grand metaphor of the Christian faith as home, away, and home again with the same changes that happen on the small or grand scale in musical compositions. A piece of music begins in the home key with the tonic chord, and then moves away to other keys, and finally rests again at the home key. Much of Western music is composed in this manner. I know this progression of chords so deeply in my body that when the music doesn't go where it's supposed to go, I feel left up in the air. When the music takes off, moves to a chord and then stays there, suspended in

---

36. Evangelical Lutheran Church in America, *Evangelical Lutheran Worship*, 317.

37. "This pregnant phrase of Bede's 'sharing the conditions' is full of wisdom. There can be effective witness without 'sharing the conditions.' Likewise, there can be no building up of the body, no encouragement, no word of discipline, no believable word of hope, no transforming love without 'sharing the conditions.'" Taylor, *In Search of Sacred Places*, 76.

midair, I long for resolution. And then usually, and more often than not, the composer takes me home, back to the tonic. In large compositions, the familiar movement of exposition, development, and recapitulation emulates the same changes as home, away, and home again. St. Irenaeus even composed his theology of incarnation and creation with this general movement in mind from exposition to development to recapitulation: God begins the creation with the basic themes, then creation emerges and develops as God continues to create with the creatures, and finally all creation will come to be what God called it to be in its final recapitulation (*anakephalaiosis*).

We must be ready to hit the road. When those of us who claim to be church sit in one place too long, becoming passive recipients of cheap grace, then things begin to decay. Martin Luther is thought to have said the following: "The church can be compared to manure. Pile it together and it stinks up the whole town; spread it out and it enriches the world." When I look for a church, I look for one that understands the need to look outward. Indeed, I have come to believe that outreach may be the most important factor in a church's success or failure. To be church means to be called outward, to be spread out into the world, for the sake of the neighbor. Always for the sake of neighbor love. That's what church means. We don't take a pilgrimage for our own religious devotion, but to learn about and share in the conditions of those in our cosmic and local neighborhoods. The trip can be to the far-flung reaches of the universe or right next door in our own backyards. But we must be willing to take the trip.

I am simultaneously a citizen of the cosmos, resident in my backyard, a pilgrim along the way, and a grateful seeker of that which is new and familiar. I inhabit several places during several times and in multiple ways. My husband embarked on a weeklong bike ride with his brother along the Mississippi River. I asked him what he will read and listen to along the way. The playlists for my life's journey would look something like this: "Detour," by Patti Page; *Appalachian Spring*, by Aaron Copland; "Morning Has Broken," sung by Cat Stevens; "Song of the Open Road," by Norman Della Joio. For those of us who claim to be church, are we ready to depart? What might our playlists be for learning and listening along the way? What prepares us to embark on the Jesus Way? Can we learn along and with not only fellow Christians but also, and maybe even more importantly, with and from other travelers whose religious and spiritual identities are not our own? I can't answer these questions for the church in abstraction; Christians are the church,

The Incarnational Marks of the Church

specific people on specific journeys. From my own pilgrimage, and being one who is on a pilgrimage of the Jesus way, I offer a few things to think about as we become church together:

1. Listen and Look. Carefully. Before you begin the journey. If you don't know where you are before you go, you won't know where you are along the way. In other words, pay attention to your own GPS location.
2. Pack ahead of time and pack along the way.
3. Travel in the places that you dwell. Pay attention to your local surroundings before you move onward.
4. Give in to the irresistibility of what calls you ahead.
5. Look back, but only if it helps to see what is ahead.
6. Take the detours.
7. Learn how to leave a place and not simply flee a place.
8. Break bread with others along the way, whether along the road to Emmaus or Wall Drug.
9. Recognize that you are on a pilgrimage in two different time zones: the time of your life, the time of the cosmos. You are on the way to becoming who you are as you travel with God.
10. Reflect on the understanding that it is God who gives us our direction. God is both the beginning and ending of our pilgrimage, a journey to and through the Alpha and Omega.
11. Learn about the limits, boundaries, or borders of your location. You cannot be present at all times and in all places. That seems to be only the divine prerogative of traveling somewhere.
12. Venture into the forgotten, hidden, scary places. Even Jesus the Christ descended to the dead. What on earth does that mean? I think it means that God goes into hell along with us, to the places that seem far deeper than we can ever imagine.
13. Cross thresholds between worlds, into the liminal spaces and thin places.
14. Dare to face the ragged edge of life.
15. And most important, share in the conditions of those who are on the journey with you.

Conclusion

In a passage from *Travels with Charley: In Search of America*, John Steinbeck writes about sharing some cognac with newfound friends on his journey: "And the few divided drops of that third there came into Rocinante a triumphant human magic that can bless a house, or a truck for that matter—nine people gathered in complete silence and the nine parts making a whole as surely as my arms and legs are part of me, separate and inseparable."[38]

Much of what I learned about church, I learned from attending Christikon (as both a camper and staffperson), from reading literature like that written by John Steinbeck, and from growing up out in Montana. I preached several times on the theme of the body of Christ, and so when I ran across this passage of Steinbeck's I thought about all kinds of communions, blessings, and bodies gathered together. As I reread Steinbeck's book again, I'm delighted at the attention he pays to the little things, to his dog's pronunciation of the consonant *f*, to the local customs and shops he encounters along the way, and to his own philosophizing about the American spirit. There is no doubt he loves the trip for its own sake; the travel to somewhere and yet to nowhere. He discovers life along the way with his companion poodle, Charley. Maybe being church also involves being on a journey. Church is about life along the way, I think. Church can be about an experiment in living that way, about that community, about providing freedom from the constraints of our crazy lives that limit our being open to others and to God. But we must discover God and church along the way, and we may find it in magic moments sharing food and drink, in compassionate embraces with those who suffer, in the companion animals who share our lives, through the hard work and adventuresome play of daily life. We aren't church already; we become church along the way. Church is both particular within the bodies of Christ that we are and cosmically as we partake in the larger body of God. Creation is the community in which we are church. There is no other place, no other church.

I have wondered why every time I read Bonhoeffer with college students and graduate students, they are so fascinated by what he has to say. It might be the integrity of his life and his message. It might be his spirituality. But what I mostly hear is their dissatisfaction with the institutional church and with the Christian faith as they have known it. Like Bonhoeffer, they

---

38. Steinbeck, *Travels with Charley*, 63.

The Incarnational Marks of the Church

find that it doesn't work: Christianity in its institutional forms does not meet people where they are. It focuses too much on another world and not enough on this one. So, when they read this quote from Bonhoeffer, they find themselves at home with his notion of faith. He wrote in July 1944: "I discovered later, and I'm still discovering right up to this moment, that it is only by living completely in this world that one learns to have faith. By this-worldliness I mean living unreservedly in life's duties, problems, successes and failures, experiences and perplexities. In so doing we throw ourselves completely into the arms of God, taking seriously, not our own sufferings, but those of God in the world. That, I think, is faith."[39] Living unreservedly, with passion and love, with service and compassion, throwing yourselves in the work of God, knowing that it is God who abides in you and you in God. That is church. At least for now.

---

39. Kelly and Nelson, eds., *A Testament to Freedom*, 510.

7

We End Where We Began

ENDINGS/BEGINNINGS

In our End
is our Beginning
tho we little note
a snowball
it gathers e thru
m
and
c squared
rolling up
the days
and
[the] years
The End
peeks through
a pain here
a creak there
a vital part slows down
needs a fix
for the heart the hip
the mind
Endings close doors

We End Where We Began

fewer miles
underfoot
Fewer rallies with
the friends, fewer
cheers with the
gang
Endings open doors
release recol-
lection
emotions
forgotten or
repressed
past scenes of
regret and joy

Unleash reflection
flattened in the living
but deeper in
remembering—
truly re-
membered
connected
densely
in the self
Beginnings
do we see them
are they noted
peeking through

Do they wane
as endings wax
or keep an even
balance
or prevail
Is beginning always there
an alarm clock heard
a new dawn
step trod
dreams visioned

The Geography of God's Incarnation

    stories heard
    lines turned on
    poet's wheel

    Our beginning
    the team
    regroups
    in
    Sobornost*
    heroics to pathos
    militants to victors
    Others' beginnings
    reach endings
    'round us
    friend here
    sib there
    Their beginnings a winning
    or
    their ending sheer loss[40]

*Sobornost—Russian idea of intense community of all people, living and dead.

    Our endings are the place and time from which we start our life. As soon as we are born, we begin a slow process of dying. This is not meant to be a morose, sad statement but merely one that states the obvious. A truth we try so hard to forget or deny. Today, the crimson maple leaves are dropping to the ground and are seized by the prairie winds, whipped into piles in my yard. Most of the trees have already shed their foliage, and the cold, brisk north wind reminds me that winter will be on its way. Fall heralds the end of summer and its warmth; it also marks the beginning of a new schoolyear. The seasons are the way that time and place come together to remind me that my life, like the patterns in the nonhuman world, are marked by life and death. This fall has been difficult again with news that colleagues and friends are struggling with cancer, signaling that endings are poignantly closer than they or any of us want to know. What sense can I make of all this, of the hope that somehow God's grace will transform death into life, to make new that which is

---

    40. Hefner, "Beginnings and Endings," April 4, 2012. This poem took shape as Hefner reflected on a friend's death.

old, and give hope where there is despair. The incarnation of God in this world is a promise that this world, in all of its rich and fragile beauty and painful sadness, is precisely where God wants to be to bring promises to fruition. As Luther remarked, it is always in this time and this place that God promises to be present for us. I yearn hopefully that these promises will come true.

I am ending where I am beginning—once again on the road to Beaver Creek with my dogs and mother in tow. As we turn off the pavement and onto the gravel road, Jack the poodle comes to life. He knows where we are going. A week ago the red, orange, and yellow leaves clung to the trees. Today they are mostly gone. Trees bare their arms to the gray skies; it smells like fall. Only the prairie grasses shimmer with remnants of color—pale yellow and an occasional red flame. Beaver Creek barely moves along the channel it has carved through the pastures. Drought has plagued the Midwest for months, and life has almost dried up. There are promises of rain this week. When we turn into Beaver Creek Nature Preserve, the dogs' tails are beating against the car windows, drumming with a rhythm of joy. They leap from the SUV and run. Walking along the paths, I pull up my coat collar. The wind is colder than I thought it would be; its sharpness cuts through my layers. Once again I walk through what I call Our Lady of Beaver Creek—this prairie preserve that has become a sanctuary for me. For a brief time, I can relax and let the grasses and trees, and the joy that the dogs exude while chasing one another, offer their words of grace to me. For I know that in the spring, after the winter snows have melted, the green will return. Endings will transform into beginnings, and that which was cold and dead will warm and return with life. Our endings are our beginnings.

Martin Luther wrote that when we arise in the morning and go to bed in the evening we should mark ourselves with the sign of the cross to remind ourselves whose we are. When I think about my friends who struggle with cancer, or the dry land that longs for water, I try to trust that this God who began all things will also bring our endings to new beginnings. The book of Revelation, placed at the very end of Christian Scripture, promises just that. The author writes:

> Then I saw a new heaven and a new earth; for the first heaven and the first earth had passed away, and the sea was no more. And I saw the holy city, the new Jerusalem, coming down out of heaven from God, prepared as a bride adorned for her husband. And I heard a loud voice from the throne saying, "See, the home of God is among mortals. He will dwell with them; they will be

The Geography of God's Incarnation

> his peoples, and God himself will be with them; he will wipe every tear from their eyes. Death will be no more; mourning and crying and pain will be no more, for the first things have passed away." And the one who was seated on the throne said, See, I am making all things new." Also he said, "Write this, for these words are trustworthy and true."[41]

That which is old will be made new, and the endings are beginnings. Death will be no more, and there will be a new heaven and earth. This is the incarnation come to life again. God's sonata, the great composition of creation—exposition, development, recapitulation. And this promise is not just for humankind but all of life, for a new heaven and a new earth. On earth as in heaven. God will dwell with us. The Word will continue to come to make a home among us.

A Lesson in Incarnation: Where West Meets East

A few weeks ago I traveled to Germany for a conference of the International Society of Science and Religion. About forty to fifty scholars from the United States and Europe met at a Lutheran conference center near the small town of Loccum. On my first walk around the area, I greeted a few people on their bikes, gazed upon a brown horse in a nearby pasture, and found the one stoplight in the town. Given the isolation of where we were situated, those of us at the conference realized that we would get to know each other well because there wasn't any other site to distract us during our brief and rather infrequent breaks from giving papers. So we drank coffee, sipped on wine, and shared meals together. One evening I sat at the table with Christopher Knight, a British scholar who converted from his Anglican tradition to Eastern Orthodoxy. I had given my paper that morning, and he reminded me again about the rich resources on the theology of the incarnation that the Eastern Orthodox tradition can offer to theologians from the Western traditions of Christianity.

I offer an example of how Western views of Christianity can seem so limited and can constrict the scope of the gospel. I often listen to Lutheran sermons, centered on justification by grace through faith alone—expositions of Martin Luther's theology. So many times Luther is interpreted with a Western lens: the point of Jesus's death is to save us from our sinful selves and forgive our sins. That's it. Period. The gospel in a forensic

---

41. Revelation 21: 1–5 (NRSV).

nutshell. This emphasis on the death of Jesus, explained with the language and metaphors of the courtroom, however, seems to only address part of the complex and messy state of our lives. There is more to life than sin. These Lutheran sermons so often focus narrowly on human bondage to sin that they eclipse the rest of creation—the place in which God dwells. What about the problems of suffering, finitude, loss, and constant grief? And not just for humans, but also for all creation that groans in travail. God promises more—that all of life, which is tired and old, will be renewed and given hope. Justification by grace is an incarnational Word that addresses the scope of all creation; for God so loved the whole creation. God will dwell here, in this place and this time, among us. It took a trip to Germany to remind me once again that while I'm rooted in the traditions of the West, I must explore other theological regions whose riches can expand my own incarnational landscape. I can enlist those scholars of the Eastern traditions, those magi who came to the one who is Incarnate, who will offer me the gifts of their wisdom.

That evening, after dinner with Christopher Knight, I opened the Amazon site on my iPad and ordered his book. It was waiting for me when I returned from Germany, and since then I have been reading the writings of the Eastern fathers, particularly of Maximos the Confessor, to expand and challenge my Western reading of incarnation. Word and words, *Logos* and *logoi*, come together to open the incarnation of God to all things. Christopher Knight writes: "These *logoi*, through inhering in each created thing, are not themselves created. They are, for Maximos, nothing other than God's presence in each thing: a manifestation of the *Logos* itself."[42] Western theologians frequently focus the lens of the incarnation through Anselm's famous question: why did God become human? This question is usually answered by an explanation that God comes in Jesus to save us from our sins, through his death on the cross.[43] However, theologians like Maximos the Confessor challenge this narrow reading with the notion that if humankind had never fallen, God would still have become incarnate in the person of Jesus Christ, simply for the sake of God's love for humankind.[44] God's home is in this world, in us, just because God likes to hang out with us!

---

42. Knight, *The God of Nature*, 98.
43. Ibid.
44. Ibid.

The Geography of God's Incarnation

So, I can take this expanded vision of the incarnation, which includes all creation, and use it to open up what it means to be created in the image of God. Knight suggested that Eastern Orthodox understandings of the incarnation might offer just this kind of theological support for a reinterpretation of the *imago Dei*. He writes: "For Maximos, this understanding led to an expansion of what Philip Sherrard has called the Greek patristic understanding of 'the universality of the Incarnation,' in which the Logos is seen as incorporating itself 'not in the body of a single human being alone but in the totality of human nature, in mankind as a whole, in creation as a whole.'"[1] Incarnations and images of God are visions of the creation's relationship to its Creator. East might meet West in the claim that all creation reflects both the Incarnation and image of God. From my conversations with Christopher Knight, I know that my vision from the West must be met by a correction from the East.

That's why on the last day of the conference in Germany when we met for Sunday Eucharist, not only did I experience the grace of God in those gathered around the table, but also I sensed a kinship with all of creation. When Fraser Watts, a psychologist and Anglican priest, presided at the Eucharist, he welcomed all of us—from Anabaptist to Orthodox, to the table to receive God's grace. In this small chapel in Loccum, Germany, at this table, God's hospitality was present for all, including, I believe, all of creation. As God dwelled in us, we resided in God—theosis came to life as it became mutual indwelling of human and divine. I want to read more of those theologians of the East, those magical magi whose wisdom leads me to the star above the Incarnate One.

When I left the shores of Germany to fly back to the United States, I knew something had happened to me. My view on the world had changed again. As I returned to Sioux Falls and the prairies of South Dakota, I came home again, but with new views. Since that conference, I have had an urge to head west again—this time not to just see the sites of the South Dakota Badlands but to read them in the texts of the Orthodox theologians. According to Kathleen Norris, the landscapes of western South Dakota have the traditions of the Eastern Orthodox fathers imbedded in them. She writes: "When a friend referred to the western Dakotas as the Cappadocia of North America, I was handed an essential connection between the spirituality of the landscape I inhabit and that of the fourth-century monastics who set up shop in Cappadocia and the

---

1. Knight, *The God of Nature*, 98.

deserts of Egypt."[2] The chalky buttes and pyramids of sediment of the Badlands offer a window onto the landscape of the Cappadocians—those desert patristic writers who have only begun to shape my understanding of Christianity. I can't travel to Turkey right now, but I can read Gregory of Nazianzus or Gregory of Nyssa in light of a landscape that would have been much like theirs. The trip to Germany reminds me that places are made from the relationships that people have with them. Bodies and places come together in incarnation.

Sacrament of Place: Body and Location Come Together

The theme of the conference in Germany was embodied cognition. I admit that I knew nothing about the field of cognitive science. Those who are in the field of embodied cognition explain that the way we see and know the world is inextricably connected to how we interact with the world. This feature of embodied cognition is called extended mind. "In this view, the mind leaks out into the world, and cognitive activity is distributed across individuals and situations. This is not your grandmother's metaphysics of mind; this is a brave new world."[3] This view challenges the Cartesian notion that our minds are inside our bodies. While this understanding of extended mind remains controversial at both scientific and philosophical levels, it has at least provoked me to think that the way we see the world is embodied, situated, and interactive. These embodied interactions might entail more than just a cause-and-effect relationship with mind, but might indeed create cognition.

At some intuitive level, I thought that the theme of this conference reminded me of my favorite aphorism of Alfred North Whitehead's that I quoted earlier: that I when I enter a room I don't say, "Hello, I'm Ann Pederson, and I brought my body with me." We are our bodies. However, in the philosophy we have inherited from Descartes, we Western Enlightenment selves have been trained to think that our minds and bodies are separate. Or from another view, we claim that our minds are nothing but the neural connections in our brains. The new fields of embodied cognition challenge both these views. We construct our minds through the bodies with which we engage the world around us. Our knowledge is

---

2. Norris, *Dakota*, 3.

3. Robbins and Aydede, "A Short Primer on Situated Cognition," in *The Cambridge Handbook of Situated Cognition*, 8.

The Geography of God's Incarnation

not only embodied; it's also situated. "The world serves not just our own minds but also our communications with other minds: a glance at the door tells a partner that it is time to leave; the salt and pepper shakers on a dinner table act as props in a dramatic retelling; here, that, and this way can be understood efficiently but only in context."[4] Or another way to put this is, "Cognition is not just situated, it is also embodied, in ways that are hard to untangle."[5] Barbara Tversky claims that spatial thinking is foundational for the other ways we talk and think in the world. The spaces we occupy shape our thoughts and perceptions about them, and so people react differently to the same space.[6]

How do we navigate in the world? Tversky explains that we do so in several ways: "The pieces can be views from experience, they can be descriptions we have heard or read, or they can be maps we have studied."[7] As we navigate the world, we also create errors. We leave out some information, can't integrate other pieces, and yet we try to create a coherent map of our world. Trevksy explains that when we talk about where we are going, we use two perspectives: the survey and the route. From a route perspective, one imagines that the person is traveling, and describes the various landmarks along the way in terms of "left, right, front, and back." From a survey perspective, the one telling about the journey takes the "bird's eye" view by locating landmarks as if "from the top" and uses terms of "north, south, east and west."[8] What is fascinating to me is that when an event looms in the far-distant future, we use the survey perception to describe how we get from here to there. When events are closer in time, we use the route perspective as our perceptual map. The ways we think about who we are have to do with how our bodies relate to where we are. This should seem so obvious. Tversky explains that "our bodies not only sense but also participate in thought; we use our bodies to locate, to refer, to measure, to arrange and rearrange, to transform. Imagination is not limited by the body and the world; it is enabled by the body and the world."[9] But what is obvious isn't always the case. The ways many Christians explain their religious experiences locates them in the inner

---

4. Tversky, "Spatial Cognition: Embodied and Situated," 201.

5. Ibid., 202.

6. Tversky writes: "Because perception and action in space differ, so conceptions of these spaces differ." Ibid., 202.

7. Ibid., 205.

8. Ibid., 207.

9. Ibid., 213.

world of a disembodied mind. Not only do the sciences of embodied and situated cognition challenge this view, but so also do the sacramental and incarnational theologies. They counter this narrow view by claiming that God is not present somewhere inside some spiritual chamber in our heart or head, but instead that God dwells in all that we are and in all with whom we are in relationship.

Each of us learns to think and communicate in, with, and under the body's relationship to the world around us. Our minds extend into and are created with by the interactions it has with its environment—from the body to those places, people, and events around the body. Perception, action, and thought create each other.[10] St. Paul's image of the body of Christ becomes much more interesting when we know that the various parts of our body and brain, and the relationships between them, construct reality. The body of Christ is both person and place. Our bodies are the relationships through which we engage the environment around us. Incarnation—God's person dwells. Divine, embodied Cognition. Where we are is after all who we are. Christians are situated—both as those who dwell in Christ and those who are on the Way.

Where Will My Travels Take Me? Tourist, Dweller, and Pilgrim

Not too long ago the lectionary Gospel text appointed for a given Sunday came from John 6. The pericope is routinely called "The Feeding of the Five Thousand." After discussing it with my colleague Richard Swanson and hearing a different sermon on the passage, I think I would change the common title of this pericope from John 6 to the following: The Transformation of tourists into pilgrims. Here is the story from John:

> After this Jesus went to the other side of the Sea of Galilee, also called the Sea of Tiberias. A large crowd kept following him, because they saw the signs that he was doing for the sick. Jesus went up the mountain and sat down there with his disciples. Now the Passover, the festival of the Jews, was near. When he looked up and saw a large crowd coming towards him, Jesus said to Philip, "Where are we to buy bread for these people to eat?" He said this to test him, for he himself knew what he was going to do. Philip answered him, "Six months' wages would not buy enough bread for each of them to get a little." One of his disciples, Andrew, Simon Peter's brother, said to him, "There is a boy here who has

10. Robbins and Aydede, "A Short Primer on Situated Cognition," 4.

The Geography of God's Incarnation

five barley loaves and two fish. But what are they among so many people?" Jesus said, "Make the people sit down." Now there was a great deal of grass in the place; so they sat down, about five thousand in all. Then Jesus took the loaves, and when he had given thanks, he distributed them to those who were seated; so also the fish, as much as they wanted. When they were satisfied, he told his disciples, "Gather up the fragments left over, so that nothing may be lost." So they gathered them up, and from the fragments of the five barley loaves, left by those who had eaten, they filled twelve baskets. When the people saw the sign that he had done, they began to say, "This is indeed the prophet who is to come into the world."

When Jesus realized that they were about to come and take him by force to make him king, he withdrew again to the mountain by himself.[11]

I have always thought this passage was just another miracle story—Jesus feeds the five thousand. But when I listened to and read this text again, and then again, I realize that Jesus feeds people who don't ask to be fed. The text never says that they are hungry.[12] In fact, they weren't following Jesus to see him break bread. They are more like religious tourists, following Jesus to see if they catch a glimpse of him healing the sick. They are excited to see the signs that he was doing. The author of the text also explains that it is Passover, a festival for which pilgrimage is made.[13] But Jesus doesn't go to Jerusalem, and those following him don't seem to have Jerusalem as a destination in mind; rather they are like tourists, out to see the sights and sites. Then when Jesus sees the crowds, he wonders how he is going to feed them even though no mention is made of their hunger. The crowds come to see Jesus heal the sick, and then instead he feeds them with barley loaves. Might they have been disappointed? Richard Swanson explains that in Mark's version of the story, the kind of bread isn't mentioned. But John notes that it is bread made of barley. "Barley makes a coarser loaf, and even poorer food. Wheat, the assumed grain, in the Gospel of Mark, makes a finer meal. But barley brings with it echoes from the life of the prophet Elijah, who fed a poor widow on barley loaves."[14] What an odd story.

11. John 6:1–15 (NRSV).
12. Swanson, *Provoking the Gospel of John*, 223.
13. Ibid., 216.
14. Ibid.

This text, in a strangely familiar way, reminds me of those times when I have pulled off on the roadside to see some weird tourist attraction, maybe even a religious shrine. That's what tourists do: they travel to get glimpses of the sites. If we place ourselves as part of the crowd, we end up becoming religious tourists—waiting and watching to see the signs Jesus will do for the sick. We aren't even hungry; we probably grabbed something at the last McDonald's. We follow Jesus up a mountain. Passover is near; why aren't we on a pilgrimage to Jerusalem? We see this event from the top of the mountain, from a birds-eye view. But when we encounter Jesus, our view is changed from the birds-eye-view of the tourist to the specific route a pilgrim might take. Just as Jesus fed those who were on the road to Emmaus, Jesus feeds us on the way, whether or not we are hungry. This Way is one of hospitality. Jesus becomes the host for our meal and feeds us. "Throughout the Gospel of John, hospitality is one of the dominant metaphor fields evoking the incarnate presence of God-with-us."[15] This reinforces the opening emphasis of John on God dwelling with us, in the dining room—sharing food together. This God is domestic. I am simultaneously a tourist, pilgrim, and resident. My ending is the beginning. I think about all those who have accompanied me along the way, and who have gone before me. No matter where I go, or how I travel, I know my home is in God. And that is just enough grace to sustain me on the next journeys that I must undertake.

---

15. O'Day, "John 6:1–15," 196–98.

Bibliography

ABC News et al. *A Hidden America: Children of the Plains*. Narrated by Diane Sawyer. 20/20. Released October 13, 2011. New York: ABC News, 2011. DVD.
"Access to Recreation." Website: Montana Fish, Wildlife & Parks. Online: http:// fwp.mt.gov/doingBusiness/reference/montanaChallenge/vignettes/access.html/.
Arnheim, Rudolf. *Visual Thinking*. Berkeley: University of California Press, 1969.
Augustana College. The Center of Western Studies. Website: http://augie.edu/cws/.
Aune, Michael. "Using the Fictions of Ole Rolvaag and Arthur Islas to Reconsider Lutheran Identity in America." *Dialog: A Journal of Theology* 42/2 (2003) 146–54.
Bartnick, Kelly. "Boom: Black Oil, Bright Future." KELO-TV. Posted on May 9, 2012. Online: http://www.keloland.com/newsdetail.cfm/boom-black-oil-bright-future/?id=131516/.
Barr, Nevada. *High Country*. New York: Berkley Books, 2005.
Batson, Michael. *Michael Batson: Travel Writer*. Website. Online: http://www.michaelbatson.co.nz/
Bottum, Joseph. "The Cold, Hard Truth." *The Wall Street Journal* (Eastern Edition). November 24, 2004, D-10.
Bouma-Prediger, Steven, and Peter Bakken, editors. *Evocations of Grace: The Writings of Joseph Sittler on Ecology, Theology, and Ethics*, by Joseph Sittler. Grand Rapids: Eerdmans, 2000.
Brown, Dee. *Bury My Heart at Wounded Knee*. New York, Holt, Rinehart & Winston, 1971.
Bryson, Bill. *The Lost Continent: Travels in Small-Town America*. New York: Harper Perennial, 1989.
"Buffalo, South Dakota." *Wikipedia*. Online: http://en.wikipedia.org/wiki/Buffalo,_South_Dakota/.
Chesapeake Bay Foundation. "No Child Left Inside." Webpage. Online: http://www.cbf.org/ncli/landing/.
Chessman, Harriet Scott. *Lydia Cassatt Reading the Morning Paper: A Novel*. New York: Penguin, 2001.
Clary, Amy. "Technonature: Wilderness and Simulation on the 'Last Frontier.'" 24/1 (2007) 51–64.
Coleman, Monica. *Making a Way Out of No Way: A Womanist Theology*. Innovations: African American Religious Thought. Minneapolis: Fortress, 2008.
Hedge-Cook, Allison Adelle. *Blood Run: Free Verse Play*. Earthworks Series. Cambridge: SALT, 2006.

Bibliography

De Blij, Harm. *The Power of Place: Geography, Destiny, and Globalization and Rough Landscape.* Oxford: Oxford University Press, 2009.

De Waal, Esther. *Every Earthly Blessing: Rediscovering the Celtic Tradition.* Harrisburg, PA: Morehouse, 1999.

———. *To Pause at the Threshold: Reflections on Living on the Border.* Harrisburg, PA: Morehouse, 2004.

Dillard, Annie. *Teaching a Stone to Talk.* New York: HarperCollins E-books, 2007.

Eck, Diana. *Darsan: Seeing the Divine Image in India.* 3rd ed. New York: Columbia University Press, 1998.

Else, Jon, director. *The Day after Trinity: Robert Oppenheimer and the Atomic Bomb.* DVD. Chatsworth, CA: Image Entertainment, 2002.

Evangelical Lutheran Church in America. *Evangelical Lutheran Worship.* Minneapolis: Augsburg Fortress, 2006.

Evangelical Lutheran Synod of Missouri, Ohio, and Other States. *The Augsburg Confession.* In *Triglot Concordia: The Symbolical Books of the Evangelical Lutheran Church: German-Latin-English.* Online: http://www.bookofconcord.org/augsburgconfession.php/.

Fischer, Robert W. "Introduction to Volume 37." *Luther's Works,* Volume 37, *Word and Sacrament* III, edited by Robert H. Fischer. Philadelphia: Fortress, 1961.

"Fly-over States." In *The Urban Dictionary.* Online: http://www.urbandictionary.com/define.php?term=fly-over+state/.

Forsberg, Michael et al. *Great Plains: America's Lingering Wild.* Chicago: University of Chicago Press, 2009.

"Foster Children Tragedy: South Dakota Historical Markers." Website: waymarkers.com/ Date Posted: 5/16/2006. Posted by: MNSearchers. Online: http://www.waymarking.com/waymarks/WMCRF_Foster_Children_Tragedy/

Francis of Assisi, Saint. "Canticle of the Sun." Translated by Bill Barrett. In *Brother Sun, Sister Moon: St. Francis's Canticle of the Creatures,* reimagined by Katherine Paterson, and illustrated by Pamela Dalton, 25–28. San Francisco: Chronicle, 2011.

Fretheim, Terrence. *Creation Untamed: The Bible, God, and Natural Disasters.* Grand Rapids: Baker Academic, 2010.

Friedman, Thomas. *The World Is Flat: A Brief History of the Twenty-First Century.* New York: Picador, 2007.

Galloway, Bryan. "Why Did Dietrich Bonhoeffer Go to America and Then Return to Germany?" Blog post on *Bonhoeffer Blog.* September 22, 2009. Online: http://bonhoefferblog.wordpress.com/2009/09/22/why-did-dietrich-bonhoeffer-go-to-america-and-then-return-to-germany/

Gilkey, Langdon. "Nature as the Image of God." *Zygon* 29 (1994) 489–505.

Gessen, Masha. *Blood Matters: From Inherited Illness to Designer Babies, How the World and I Found Ourselves in the Future of the Gene.* Orlando: Harcourt, 2008.

Hamma, Robert. W. *Landscapes of the Soul: A Spirituality of Place.* Notre Dame, IN: Ave Maria Press, 1999.

Hefner, Philip. *The Human Factor: Evolution, Culture, and Religion.* Minneapolis: Fortress, 1993.

———. *Technology and Human Becoming.* Minneapolis: Fortress, 2003.

———. "Beginnings and Endings." Unpublished poem. Written April 4, 2012.

———. "Soul Shape." Unpublished poem. 2012.

Bibliography

Highland, Chris, compiler and editor. *Meditations of John Muir: Nature's Temple*. Berkley: Wilderness Press, 2001.
Iyer, Pico. "The Joy of Quiet." *The New York Times*. December 29, 2011. Online: http://www.nytimes.com/2012/01/01/opinion/sunday/the-joy-of-quiet.html?pagewanted=all&_r=0/
Johnson, Dirk. "The Nation: Forget the Last Picture Shows: In Some Towns the Bank and the High School Are Closing Too." *The New York Times*. August 18, 1991, A.2. Online: http://www.nytimes.com/1991/08/18/weekinreview/nation-forget-last-picture-show-some-towns-bank-high-school-are-closing-too.html/.
John Whirlwind Soldier, director. *More Than That*. Video featuring students of the Sioux Reservation's county high school. Online: http://www.youtube.com/watch?v=FhribaNXr7A/.
Kazantzakis, Nikos. *Report to Greco*. Oxford: Cassirer, 1965.
Keller, Rosanne. *Pilgrim in Time: Mindful Journeys to Encounter the Sacred*. Collegeville, MN: Liturgical, 2006.
Kelly, Geffrey B., and F. Burton Nelson, editors. *A Testament to Freedom: The Essential Writings of Dietrich Bonhoeffer*. San Francisco: HarperSanFrancisco, 1995.
Knight, Christopher C. *The God of Nature: Incarnation and Contemporary Science*. Theology and the Sciences. Minneapolis: Fortress, 2007.
Lane, Belden. *Landscapes of the Sacred: Geography and Narrative in American Spirituality*. Expanded ed. Baltimore: Johns Hopkins University Press, 2002.
"Lost Bird Story Summary." Website: *Lost Bird of Wounded Knee*. Online: http://www.sdpb.org/Lostbird/summary.asp/.
Maclean, Norman. *Young Men & Fire*. Chicago: University of Chicago Press, 1992.
McCune, Marianne, correspondent. "Rehabilitating Juarez's International Image." On the Media. Transcript posted June 22, 2012. Online: http://www.onthemedia.org/2012/jun/22/placeholderfor-juarez-image-change-slug/transcript/.
Metaxas, Eric. *Bonhoeffer: Pastor, Martyr, Prophet, Spy*. Foreword by Timothy J. Keller. Nashville: Nelson, 2010.
Murphy, Tim. "Where the West Begins (or Doesn't)." Blog: *Mother Jones*. August 25, 2010. Online: http://www.motherjones.com/road-trip-blog/2010/08/where-west-begins/.
Norris, Kathleen. *Dakota: A Spiritual Geography*. New York: Tichnor & Fields, 1993.
O'Day. Gail R. "John 6:1-15." *Interpretation* 57 (2003) 196–98.
Pederson, Ann. "Soteriological Motifs in the Theologies of Kazantzakis and Luther." In *God's Struggler: Religion in the Writings of Nikos Kazantzakis*, edited by Darren T. N. Middleton and Peter Bien, 93–111. Macon, GA: Mercer University Press, 1996.
———. "The Juxtaposition of Naturalistic and Christian Faith: Reappraising the Natural From within a Different Theological Lens." In *All That Is: A Naturalistic Faith for the Twenty-First Century*, edited by Philip Clayton, 119–29. Minneapolis: Fortress 2007.
Peterson, Eugene H. *A Long Obedience in the Same Direction: Discipleship in an Instant Society*. 20th anniversary ed. Downers Grove, IL: InterVarsity, 2000.
Peterson, Gregory. "Imago Dei." In *Encyclopedia of Science and Religion*, edited by J. Wentzel van Huyssteen et al., 449–50. New York: Macmillan Reference, USA, 2003.
Pozin, Ilya. "7 Things Highly Productive People Do." Online: http://www.inc.com/ilya-pozin/7-things-highly-productive-people-do.html/.

Bibliography

"The Process." On *The Saint John's Bible*. Website. Online: http://www.saintjohnsbible.org/process/.

"Record Group 4: Hague Synod." Luther Seminary. Website. Online: http://www.luthersem.edu/archives/Collections/4-Hauge.aspx/.

Reynolds, Meredith. "You Transplanted a Vine from Egypt . . . It Took Root and Filled the Land." Senior Sermon. Spring 2012. Augustana College, Sioux Falls, SD. Chapel of Reconciliation.

Robbins, Jim. "The Ecology of Disease." *Sunday Review*. *The New York Times*. July 14, 2012. Online: http://www.nytimes.com/2012/07/15/sunday-review/the-ecology-of-disease.html?r=1&pagewanted=all

Robbins, Philip, and Murat Aydede. *The Cambridge Handbook of Situated Cognition*. Cambridge: Cambridge University Press, 2009.

Rogness, Michael. "Proclaiming the Gospel on Mars Hill." *Word and World* 27 (2007) 274–94.

Rohr, Richard. *Falling Upward: A Spirituality for the Two Halves of Life*. San Francisco: Jossey-Bass, 2011.

———. "Following the Mystics." Daily devotional. In *Following the Mystics through the Narrow Gate . . . Seeing God in All Things*, by Richard Rohr et al. DVD. Albaquerque: Center for Action and Contemplation, 2009.

Ryu, Chesung Justin. "Silence as Resistance: A Postcolonial Reading of the Silence of Jonah in Jonah 4:1–11. *Journal for the Study of the Old Testament* 34/2 (2009) 195–218.

Sanford Research. "Sanford Applied Biosciences." Webpage. Online: http://www.sanfordresearch.org/researchcenters/appliedbiosciences/.

Schactman, Brian A. "To Frack or Not to Frack: N. Dakota's Dilemma." February 6, 2012. Online: http://www.cnbc.com/id/46282286/.

Schmidt-Grimminger, Delf C. et al. "HPV Infection among Rural American Indian Women and Urban White Women in South Dakota: An HPV Prevalence Study." *BMC Infections Diseases*. 2011. 11:252. Online: http://www.biomedcentral.com/1471-2334/11/252/.

Sheldrake, Philip. *Spaces for the Sacred: Place, Memory, and Identity*. Baltimore: Johns Hopkins University Press, 2001.

Sittler, Joseph. "Called to Unity." In *Evocations of Grace: The Writings of Joseph Sittler on Ecology, Theology, and Ethics*, edited by Steven Bouma-Prediger and Peter Bakken, 38–50. Grand Rapids: Eerdmans, 2000.

———. *Essays on Nature and Grace*. Philadelphia: Fortress, 1972.

———. *Gravity & Grace: Reflections and Provocations*. Edited by Linda-Marie Delloff. Minneapolis: Augsburg, 1986.

Skinner, Matt. "Commentary on Acts 17:22-31. Commentary on First Reading. Online: http://www.workingpreacher.org/preaching_print_aspx?commentary_id=886/.

"South Dakota Highway 44." *Wikipedia*. Online: http://en.wikipedia.org/wiki/South_Dakota_Highway_44/.

The South Dakota Parks & Wildlife Foundation. "The Blood Run Native American Historical Site." Website. Online: http://parkswildlifefoundation.org/project/BloodRun.aspx/.

Staunton, Ruth, and Dorothy Louise Keur. *Jerkline to Jeep: A Brief History of the Upper Boulder*. Harlotown, MT: Times Clarion, 1975.

Bibliography

Stawicki, Elizabeth. "A Haunting Legacy: Canton Insane Asylum for American Indians." "News and Features." Minnesota Public Media. Website. Posted on Decemer 9, 1997. Online: http://news.minnesota.publicradio.org/features/199712/09_stawickie_asylum/.

Stegner, Wallace. *Where the Bluebird Sings to the Lemonade Springs: Living and Writing in the West.* New York: Penguin, 1992.

Steinbeck, John. *Travels with Charley.* New York: Viking, 1969.

Storm, Jill. "Caring, Context, and Otherness." Lecture. Senior Capstone Class, Spring, 2012. Augustana College, Sioux Falls, SD.

Swanson, Richard W. *Provoking the Gospel of Mark: A Storyteller's Commentary.* Cleveland: Pilgrim, 2005.

———. *Provoking the Gospel of John: A Storyteller's Commentary, Years A, B & C.* Provoking the Gospel Storytelling Commentary. Cleveland: Pilgrim, 2010.

Taylor, Barbara Brown. *An Altar in the World: A Geography of Faith.* New York: HarperOne, 2009.

Taylor, Daniel. *In Search of Sacred Places: Looking for Wisdom on Celtic Holy Islands.* Saint Paul: Bog Walk Press, 2005.

Tickle, Phyllis. "An Assessment of Great Worth." June 5, 2012. *The Emergent Village Voice* on *Patheos.* Online: http://www.patheos.com/blogs/emergentvillage/2012/06/an-assessment-of-great-worth/

Tiede, David L. "The God Who Made the World." *Currents in Theology and Mission* 33/1 (2006) 52–62.

Tippett, Krista, producer. "Ethics and the Will of God: Interview with Martin Doblmeier." *On Being.* Aired on February 2, 2006. Distributed by American Public Media.

Transova Genetics. Website. "Vision, Mission, and Values." Online: http://www.transova.com/welcome.html/.

"Tribal Leader Opposes Proposed Fracking Rule." *Bismarck Tribune*, May 9, 2012. Online: http://bismarcktribune.com/bakken/tribal-leader-opposes-proposed-fracking-rule/article_24f0d3da-99e7-11e1-86a1-0019bb2963f4.html/

Tschesnokoff, Peter. "Salvation Is Created." On *What Child Is This?: The St. Olaf Christmas Festival, Vol. 3*. Recorded by St. Olaf College choral ensembles in December 1983. CD released in 1991. St. Olaf Records E 1839.

Turkle, Sherry. *Alone Together: Why We Expect More from Technology and Less from Each Other.* New York: Basic Books, 2011.

Tversky, Barbara. "Spatial Cognition: Embodied and Situated." In *The Cambridge Handbook of Situated Cognition*, edited by Philip Robbins and Murat Aydede, 201–16. Cambridge: Cambridge University Press, 2009.

"Waymarking FAQs." Waymarking. Website. Online: http://www.waymarking.com/help/faq.aspx/.

Wheelwright, Jeffrey. *The Wandering Gene and the Indian Princess: Race, Religion, and DNA.* New York: Norton, 2012.

White, Damine F., and Chris Wilbert. *Technonatures: Environments, Technologies, Spaces and Places in the Twenty-First Century.* Environmental Humanities. Waterloo, ON: Wilfrid Laurier University Press, 2009.

Williams, Terry Tempest. *Refuge: An Unnatural History of Family and Place.* New York: Vintage, 1991.

Zehr, Howard. *The Little Book of Contemplative Photography: Seeing with Wonder, Respect, and Humility.* Intercourse, PA: Good Books, 2005.

www.ingramcontent.com/pod-product-compliance
Lightning Source LLC
Chambersburg PA
CBHW030856170426
43193CB00009BA/634